Acclaim for B~~~~

Teachers are always looking for practical ideas they can implement immediately in their classrooms for positive change. Nick's first-hand experience with PBL makes this book a must have for educators who are ready to take that next step for students to demonstrate understanding & mastery through projects (& not poster boards).

- Sherry Gick
Teacher-Librarian

Nicholas is my go-to expert on Project Based Learning and we brought him into our school several years ago to lead our in-service on PBL that was very successful. I am excited to share *Beyond the Poster Board* with my ELA teachers and I know it will be a resource they will embrace. As I was reading, I couldn't help but think of all of the ELA teachers I've worked with over the years who would love to dig into the ideas and resources presented in this book.

- Tiffany Whitehead
Director of Library at Episcopal School
of Baton Rouge

You know you want to immerse your students in collaboration, that stretches their critical thinking and gets them creating and communicating in authentic ways, so you need to try project-based learning. *Beyond the Poster Board* is the book that will help you start down that path.

- Jen Roberts
ELA Classroom teacher and
co-author of *Power Up: Making the Shift
to 1:1 Teaching and Learning.*

Get ready to rip up your trifolds! *Beyond the Poster Board* is the quintessential guide for any educator looking to delve into meaningful project work with their students. Provenzano prepares the reader for the "structured chaos" of project-based learning through the gradual release of "Recipe Projects" and "Tool-Specific Projects" to more student-driven learning experiences such as "Open PBL with Teacher Objectives" and Genius Hour or 20 Time. BTPB even tackles the topics of mentors, public speaking, and popular tools, supplies, and materials! Jam-packed with real-life student examples of PBL projects, the book itself models how purposeful pedagogy and STEAM can thrive together! Prepared to be inspired!

- Jessica L. Williams
@JLenore24
Technology Integration
Specialist/Library Media Specialist
Manchester, CT

There are lots of resources about project-based learning, but few go into the strategies and logistics of planning, leading, and assessing a project-based learning class as in *Beyond the Poster Board*. Full of real classroom examples, resources, and strategies, *Beyond the Poster Board* is great for the ELA teacher interested in project-based learning.

- Heather Lister
@heathermlister,
Chief Education Officer,
Construct Learning, Slytherin

Nicholas Provenzano's newest book provides teachers with practical approaches to provide authentic learning opportunities to stretch student learning and revitalize the "poster" project.

- Alaina Laperouse
ELA Teacher, Central Community Schools

Educators are teaching in an age where authentic learning needs to be at the heart every classroom. Nick thoughtfully and elegantly lays out how educators can redefine methods of demonstrating student understanding in more authentic way. Looking back on his own experience and the experience of others he masterfully guides readers on a journey to transform teaching and learning in any classroom. This book should be in every educator's library!

- Steven W. Anderson
Digital Learning and Relationship
Evangelist @web20classroom

What I love about this book is that it focuses on real-world reading, research, writing and deep student reflection which all have a home in the ELA curriculum. The sustained inquiry and opportunity for students to have a voice teaches learners to THINK and ACT.

- Kristin Ziemke
Author of *Read the World*

Nicholas is one of the most passionate educators I know. He always puts his students first and has always been an advocate for student voice. He has been my mentor for years around all things PBL. His easy to read book will be your number go-to resource in your amazing journey into authentic learning with project-based learning.

- Tanya Avrith
Adobe Education Evangelist

BEYOND THE POSTERBOARD

Project-Based Learning in the
English Language Arts Classroom

NICHOLAS
PROVENZANO

BLEND
Blend Education
PO Box 5953
Salem, OR 97304

ISBN: 978-1-7341725-4-6

Dedication

I dedicate this book to all the students who trusted me when I came up with crazy, and sometimes terrible, projects for them to explore, grow, and learn. You helped me learn what is best for students and for myself as a teacher. I would not be where I am without all of you.

Table of Contents

WHO IS THIS

Who Is This Guy?

Wow! Thanks for buying my book, or at least, picking it up and reading this first page. I wanted to say hello and tell you a little about myself in the hopes you will have a better understanding of where I am coming from and how my experience as an English Language Arts (ELA) teacher for 15+ years shaped my views on project-based learning (PBL) in the classroom.

Whenever I read an education book, sit in a session, or am at a keynote, I always ask myself, "Why should I listen to this person?" I feel it is so important to know a person's background and experiences if they are about to talk to me or I'm about to read their book, especially if it is supposed to influence my practices as a teacher. That is why I am always upfront with my experiences when I write or speak. Here is a little about myself if you are interested.

"Why should I listen to this person?"

I've been an educator for over 15 years, and the majority of those years I was a high school English literature teacher. From there, I moved to a position as a makerspace director and technology coordinator. That may seem like a crazy move for an English teacher, but it made sense for someone who earned his master's degree in educational technology and spent his years as an English teacher focusing on PBL and building makerspaces. I've written a few bestselling books over the years on using technology and makerspaces and have presented in places from Iceland to Singapore with lots of places in between. I work with individual teachers, school districts, universities, and even the state department of education groups.

I've been recognized as the Teacher of the Year by ISTE (International Society of Technology in Education) and MACUL (Michigan Association of Computer Users in Learning) and have a few certifications to broaden my understanding in different areas, namely, Google Certified Innovator, Raspberry Pi Certified Educator, littleBits Lead Educator, TED Ed Innovative Educator, Microsoft Minecraft Mentor, Adobe Education Leader, and Dungeon Master Level 5.

The last thing I want to note is that the things I'm going to share were either done by me in my classroom or by teachers I've worked with in their classroom. These are relevant examples in this book that you can use in your classroom, knowing that they have been tested with real students in real learning environments. That is what I plan to share with all of you in this book—that and some super casual nerd references because I simply can't help myself.

CHAPTER
1

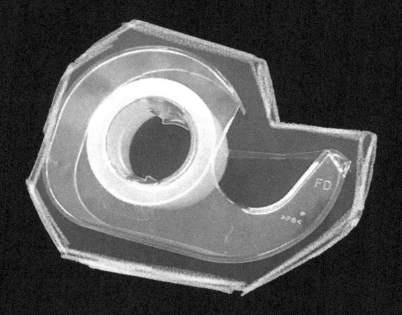

WHAT IS PROJECT-BASED LEARNING?

The Buck Institute for Education (BIE), an amazing organization filled with tremendous resources, defines PBL as "a teaching method in which students gain knowledge and skills by working for an extended period of time to investigate and respond to an authentic, engaging, and complex question, problem, or challenge."[1] This is a good working definition for BIE. They went further and created Seven Essentials Project Design Elements of PBL that are also worth noting:

1. Challenging Problem or Question
2. Sustained Inquiry
3. Authenticity
4. Student Voice and Choice
5. Reflection
6. Critique and Revision
7. Public Product

Challenging Problem or Question

The students are given projects that focus on a specific question or problem that they need to address. What this looks like will vary from class to class and grade to grade. As the teacher, you are the one that is best suited to determine the level of the problem or question that needs to be addressed by the students.

Sustained Inquiry

For the project, students are given time to dive deeply into the project. This usually involves research and discussion. If the students spend the vast majority of their time on the arts and craft portion of the project, then the driving question should be reevaluated.

Authenticity

The project should be meaningful to the student. This one is tough because some students fight connecting to classroom content. Sometimes, the students connect through the project, and the authenticity shows up on its own. We always want students to connect to the content and how it relates to their lives in some way. It takes veteran teachers to become very good at finding different ways to connect content to students. With every new group of students, there are new challenges of making content authentic. If it seems tough at first, that means you are doing it right. It will get easier with time. Do not give up!

Student Voice and Choice

When building the project, where do students have an opportunity to decide what the project will look like and how they might add some of their own ideas to their project? This is about ownership. If students feel like they own the project, they are more likely to engage in the project.

Reflection

There should always be time worked into class to reflect on what was covered. This should not be limited to projects. Discuss what works and what does not work. Be open to feedback and see how things can be improved for next time.

Critique and Revision

This does not have to be a formal process, but it can be. As students are working on the project, be active around the room to check in on student work, and offer feedback on what they are doing. Have students explain why they are taking a certain approach and offer tips to support their chosen plan.

Public Product

This one has me on the fence. While I am fully supportive of sharing students work and creating a larger audience, I do not believe that forgoing public products eliminates the work as an example of PBL. Not all projects are meant to be shared publicly. For me, "public" can mean the classroom. Assignments are usually designed for an audience of one (the teacher) but presenting in class does provide a larger audience and can impact the student's understanding of the product they presented.

While this is a solid definition of PBL and a reliable list of ideas, I'm not the biggest fan of strict definitions. They can unintentionally exclude pretty awesome ideas because they don't fit a narrow view of what something is supposed to be. There will be elements of this book that PBL purists will say is not true PBL because the question is not complex enough, the project is not long enough and doesn't require much depth of knowledge from the student, or some other nonsense.

I'm here to tell you that PBL is not about the right or wrong way to implement it in your classroom. Some ways are better and offer more freedom to students, but not all teachers are ready to go that route right away. So, before you get frustrated over the examples I give and the categories I break PBL into because they don't fit the definition that might have been shared at some Professional Development sessions a few years back, understand that I'm sharing practices with you that have worked for years and has led to a great amount of student engagement, even from the students who tend to struggle most in class.

So, what is my overarching definition of PBL?

Students creating something over a specified time to demonstrate an understanding of a specific idea(s) that is chosen by the teacher and/or student and sharing it with the community when it is completed.

I like this definition because it incorporates the elements of the Buck Institute's seven ideas but is broad enough for teachers to explore and see what other options fit best for them. The more a definition boxes in a teacher, the less likely they are to try something new. My definition gives teachers the wiggle room to try different things. If it doesn't fit just right, you can nudge it one way or the other until it fits the best way for you and your students.

By implementing PBL into the classroom, teachers are empowering students to explore what they truly know about a topic and to use their own skill set to demonstrate that understanding to others.

Why PBL in the Classroom?

The next part after explaining the *what*, is explaining the *why*. This is always a tough one because every teacher has a very different type of class, and the reasons to try PBL in their classrooms are not the same. The reason why PBL is so great in the classroom is because all classrooms are different, and PBL allows for the most differentiation of lessons. PBL is not going to take precious time away from writing or reading. It is going to convert that time into reading and writing with a more specific purpose while exploring complex ideas related to the course content. When the students have something driving the reading and writing that interests them, they will engage more fully and strengthen those skills during the project. It is ok to be skeptical of bringing a new approach to instruction into your classroom, but do not believe in the myths of PBL that are out there.

Myth 1: Students do all of the work, and the teacher just sits and grades during class.

This is the most common myth surrounding PBL. There is this idea that PBL is used by teachers as a break from teaching so they can catch up on grading. This has always driven me nuts because I have found that the best PBL lessons keep me even more active in class than a traditional writing assignment or a class discussion. I'm not saying that a teacher has never sat at their desk and graded papers while students colored poster boards, but great PBL has the teacher up and moving around the classroom.

Myth 2: Group work in projects is not fair to the students who do all the work and allows too many students to skate by without demonstrating what they know.

This is an interesting take on PBL because it seems to ignore the fact that the lesson the teacher designed allows for this type of manipulation. If the project can truly be done well by one person for an entire group, why is it a group project? Also, who chose the groups? I will go into group work later in the book, but the fear of lazy students should speak more to the assignment and less about the students.

Myth 3: What is going to stop students from just doing the same type of project over and over again? That's not real learning.

I have a mixed set of feelings about this statement. I used to run my class in a way that would require students to use a different medium for every project. I believed, like many others, that this was good for students because it forced them to explore other mediums and help them grow. However, I began to think about other creators and all of the amazing things in the world we would not have if they were told they could only paint a certain way once or sing a certain type of music once. Creators evolve over time and at their own pace. Students will do the same. Also, I'm not assessing their use of the tool, I'm assessing their understanding of the material covered in class. The medium should not matter.

Myth 4: PBL in the classroom takes away valuable writing time.

This has been brought to me as a worry before, but PBL doesn't have to take away valuable writing time. One of the things I try to get students to understand about writing is that it is best when they have a purpose. Writing an essay because I told them to is not a good enough purpose. Writing a reflection piece on their project does give students a purpose. It provides much more insight into their process of creation, and it shows even more depth of understanding of the content than just a project on its own. I have also found that informal writing helps the students who struggle to write because it allows them to work on their ideas instead of the nitty-gritty of grammar. (Editor's note: Grammar is important. However, for students who have trouble putting any thoughts to paper, just getting them to write freely and without anxiety is a much bigger concern than split infinitives or dangling modifiers.)

If you have heard any other myths, write them down and shoot me an email or a tweet, and I can add them to a post or the next edition of the book.

Project-Based Learning as a Form of Assessment

Let's talk about assessments for a moment. Probably one of the most difficult parts of a teacher's life is the idea of finding the perfect assessment that will tell you exactly what every single student in your class knows and doesn't know. The white whale of the perfect assessment has driven many teachers mad. When we look at assessments across the country, there is one main factor that drives assessments, and it is the worst thing in the entire galaxy.

Time.

Assessments have been devised simply to make assessing faster, not better. Truly think about a 50-question multiple-choice test in a 45-minute class period. What the heck are you truly trying to assess in forcing a student to rapidly answer more than a question a minute? These tests are designed to be quick and dirty ways to gather data on students, and now, teachers. It has led to a terrible testing nation that is driving students away from creative thinking and people away from the education profession—well, that and low pay, terrible funding structures, disrespectful attitudes toward the profession, out of pocket expenses every year—wait, where was I? Oh ya. Multiple-choice tests are the worst.

"Multiple-choice tests are the worst."

Multiple-choice tests are actually incredibly difficult to write and contain inherent writer bias. They also do not necessarily assess important things. They are not designed to truly find out what someone knows. They are designed to roughly find out what a large group of people know very quickly. Do you know what the incorrect answers on a multiple-choice test are called?

Distractors.

The wrong answers are designed to trick a person into putting the wrong answer on the test. What type of messed up form of assessment is that? Let's not even dive into the fact that humans form patterns all the time whether we realize it or not, and these types of tests are the easiest to cheat.

The worst part of all of this is the fact that we all pretty much know this, but we throw up our hands and figure someone else will fix it. So, how has that gone for us? I lived in the world of using large bubble sheets to assess my students, and it got to a point where I started to see some of my most engaged students struggle, just like I did as a student, with timed multiple-choice tests. I knew they knew the material when we discussed it in class, but they did not do well on these tests. I found myself curving exams and adjusting grades because I knew the exams were not providing me with accurate data. It was at that point I really started to explore alternate forms of assessment with the simple mission of finding out what my students knew.

Portfolios and Project-Based Learning

If the multiple-choice test is the quick and dirty way to assess someone, portfolios are on the opposite end of the spectrum. Portfolios are long-term commitments to student growth. Keeping track of all the student work that demonstrates student understanding and growth over time is not an easy thing to do and is viewed as completely impossible in our educational system. However, many ELA teachers have been keeping portfolios for their students for years. Writing journals that hold a year's worth of writing is a type of portfolio. Sometimes, just a Manila folder in the classroom where students put their assessed work in becomes a portfolio of their work over the course of the year. Hopefully, time is given to students to assess their growth over time and share what they think.

One of my favorite things to do with my students was to start the school year with a pretty simple writing assignment. I had not taught anything yet. I just wanted to find out what they knew and how they wrote so I could set up my writing instruction for the year. I gave the students a night to write three paragraphs to turn in the next day to me and I would spend the next couple of days marking the papers and making notes on common mistakes that needed to be covered over the course of the year. I would pass the writing back to the students and go over the issues I saw. I collected the papers and put them in a drawer. I told my students one thing about writing moving forward.

"I am not going to turn all of you into 'A' writers. However, I will help all of you become better writers by June. As long as you focus on improvement, you will have a great year writing."

Fast forward to June and the students were receiving their last paper of the year back, and I added their paper from September. The laughs and gasps from students as they held their papers side by side was hilarious. One student even said, "I can't believe I turned this in!" I smiled and replied, "Ya, that is what I thought at the time." The students would then have an open discussion about the growth in their writing, and their final exam would be a reflection piece on their growth as a reader and a writer. (*Editor's note:* Don't get me started on final exams. The idea that a large percentage of a student's grade is based on one 90-minute assessment, usually multiple-choice, is such a cheap way to assess students. It is fundamentally wrong, and it is something that needs to change.)

The reason I'm spending time on portfolios is because PBL fits really well into this model of assessments. The artifacts that students create can be saved physically or digitally along with their written assessments. This truly allows the students, teacher, and parent to see how a student has grown over the course of a set period and truly demonstrates what a student knows. The big-time goal is to create a portfolio that follows a student from year to year. Imagine a student in grade 8 looking at their writing from grade 1 or grade 5. Education is about growth, not hitting randomly assigned age benchmarks for reading, writing, math, etc.

Assessing Projects in Project-Based Learning

"How do you grade student projects if they are all so different?"

This is a question I often receive when I present on PBL. It's not our fault that we worry about grades. It is part of the system that has been in place for decades and decades, and many of us feel very beholden to grades and grading. This is because our states have decided to create laws that revolve around how students are graded. Schools require letter grades for assessments or large end of term assessments. It is not easy to work around all of the regulations regarding student assessment, but I feel I have found a nice middle ground that allows for meaningful feedback to students and letter grades for the administration.

Rubrics to the Rescue!

One of the things I needed to do was find a way to assess my students so I could enter grades into the district required gradebook and to provide meaningful feedback to students to show them where they are strong and where they need some work. I do not claim to be a rubric expert, and my first rubrics were terrible, but I feel I have grown over the years and have rubrics that support student growth, and that is what I look for in a solid rubric. Throughout the book, I will share some different lessons and rubrics. Some will be good, some will be bad, and some will be straight up embarrassing. My favorite student-created rubrics I will not be able to share because they are lost to the sands of time. I will provide a framework to help you create a system that allows students to create their own rubrics. Don't worry. It is not as scary as it seems.

Different Types of Projects in Project-Based Learning

One of the things that is important to note is that there are different types of projects that live under the umbrella of PBL. Some people might say that these project types are not a part of PBL, and they are correct if they believe in a hard, black and white definition. As I said earlier, I do not. I see PBL on more of a spectrum, and these are the different types of projects that live on that spectrum. Some of the project types are perfect for all situations, and others are only for certain types of lessons. I will cover them all and provide specific examples of how they were used in class. I will include a list of things that the teacher and student are responsible for in each project type. These expectations will be similar in some areas, but vastly different in others.

CHAPTER

2

THE
RECIPE
PROJECT

The recipe project is so named because it is a type of project in which the teacher outlines all of the things the students have to do to complete the project and receive full credit. Students are given little to no freedom to adjust the project to support their skill set. Many teachers give recipe projects as assignments and think they are living deeply in the PBL world, but sadly, this type of project is on the fringes of the PBL spectrum. Let's look at the responsibilities of students and teachers in this type of project.

Students	Teachers
Follow the directions exactly as they were written.	Create all of the requirements on the front end of the assignment.
Complete all of the work in the allotted time.	Answer questions pertaining to the handout given to the students.
Create a project that looks practically identical to every other project turned in to the teacher.	Grade the assignment when the students are done.
Use whatever skill set the teacher determined will be needed to complete the project.	May or may not use a rubric.
Focus on checking boxes to finish the required elements of the project.	Maintain all the decision-making power.
Do not have decision-making power.	

You will notice that the work for the teacher is truly done at the end, when the students submit their project. Recipe projects tend to be the same year after year because the teacher created the lesson once and has just been making copies of it from one year to the next. The grading happens at the end, when the students submit their work or present in class, and the teacher may or may not use a rubric. In a recipe project, there is very little interaction between the teacher and student during the project.

The students are focused solely on completing the task set forth by the teacher. A recipe project is more about compliance than it is about assessing understanding. Students are required to use all of the tools outlined by the teachers and do the assignment as accurately as possible to receive full credit. Student imagination is barely needed to complete this task. When the students turn in the project, those that were forced outside of their skill set will do terribly while the other students will receive higher grades, more accolades from the teacher, and possibly have their work displayed in class.

The power structure is maintained in a recipe project. The teacher dictates all of the requirements, and the students are supposed to follow all of the rules. One of the reasons that the recipe project is so common is because it conforms to the traditional model of education, which leaves the teacher with all of the power and the students with none. Giving up control of part of a class to the students is a scary thing for teachers. The fear of failure in giving students autonomy to create their own projects is what keeps many teachers living in the recipe project portion of the PBL spectrum.

Many teachers start their PBL journey with a recipe project, but it should not be the end. The problem with the recipe project is that it is a bad long-term instructional tool. Recipe projects do not always assess student understanding, but their ability to follow directions. This is where PBL turns sour.

The Transcendentalist Poster Board

I was a new teacher, and I really wanted to shake things up in the English department at my first job. I told myself I wasn't going to do things the way they were always done, and my kids were going to learn with tests *and* projects. I thought I had come up with the most creative project in the history of projects and held on to this belief for many years.

Here is an example of what *not* to do.

I have always been a fan of the transcendentalists and think the transcendentalist unit in my class is important for the students in their Sophomore year as they try and figure out who they are and what they want out of life. I came up with this idea that would have students take pictures in nature and connect those photos to quotes from the different readings we covered over the previous two weeks. The students would take those photos, print them out, write out the quotes underneath them, and present them to the class. That was it. That was the entire assignment. I was proud of this. I was super proud when I moved from a physical poster board to a digital one with Glogster. Not only was my lesson amazing and engaging, but it was also better for the environment. Ugh. Here is the actual assignment sheet I gave students.

Walden Pond Photo Essay

Take a series of photographs of nature during different times of the day and try to find visual representations of how Thoreau felt while he lived at Walden Pond. Use quotations from his essay as captions for your pictures.

Requirements:

- A minimum of 6 photographs must be used to complete the project. (10 pts each)
- Each photograph must have a caption that is a quote from his essay (5 pts each)
  - List the line number the quote can be found on.
- Pictures cannot be taken from the Internet or magazines.
- The project must be placed on a poster board and look presentable. (10 pts)
- This project is due on _____.
- If you have any questions, please see me as soon as possible.

This was the entire assignment. I had the set requirements for the entire assignment. Students did not have much choice outside the color of the poster board. Here are some things that stand out to me based on this project alone.

- The project was worth 100 points. This does not mean much out of context, but in this context 100 points was also the standard amount for full essays. It is a crazy scale for an assignment.

- I was giving 10% of their grade to just have a picture. That's it. That's worth 10 points.
- Copying a quote from a book to a poster board was worth 5%.
- Just turning in something that looked nice would get you 10%.

This is crazy. I gave this assignment for many years. Students would be rewarded with the same amount of points as a perfect essay—a complex essay with depth that takes multiple days to write, proofread, and rewrite was worth the same in the gradebook as taking six pictures in your backyard and adding quotes from a book. This is embarrassingly bad, but I don't mind sharing that here. We all have bad lessons, and this is not the type of book in which I am going to pretend that every lesson I have ever made is gold.

I finally started to ask myself, "What am I assessing?" When I looked at my projects, it really changed my view of this assignment and many others I gave out in class. I needed another lesson to replace this bad recipe project, and I worked with another teacher and created the following assignment.

Transcendental Society Group Project

Objective: To create a society based off of the ideas discussed throughout the transcendentalist unit. Use the transcendentalist pieces (examples "Walden," "Self-Reliance," "Psalm of Life," "Dead Poets Society," etc.) as a guide when creating your community.

Requirements:

- Self-selected groups of 3–5 people. (You will receive a group grade, so choose wisely.)
- All projects must be completed by November 17. All groups must be prepared to present on that day.
- While working in your groups, you will be judged on how you adhere to the transcendentalist beliefs (i.e., participation grade), while you create your community. You must be accepting of other individuals' beliefs, confident in your ideas, and use your time effectively, etc.
- Your community must focus on the following transcendentalist beliefs:
    o a reliance on one's self for true happiness
    o an emphasis on nature
    o an importance of minimal government intervention
    o a belief that humans are innately good
    o a life simply lived without distractions
    o a celebration of the individual
- You can present your society in whichever way matches your skillset (NO ESSAYS):
    o PowerPoint / Slideshows
    o Movie
    o Scrapbook
    o Brochure
    o Website
    o Newspaper
    o Etc.

While creating your society, you must complete all of the following tasks:

1. Select a name for your society. You may create a name with some meaning (from something you already know) or come up with an acronym.

2. Design and create a flag or crest using colors and symbols to illustrate the values of your society. Provide a detailed explanation for the symbols, colors, etc. used in designing your flag or crest.

3. Explain the kinds of work your society would encourage its citizens to engage in. Create example job descriptions.

4. Provide a map of your town showing landmarks/buildings and other features important to your society. (Would it be a rural society, an urban society, an island? A combination?)

5. Describe at least five behaviors your society would deem inappropriate/criminal behaviors. Then explain how your society would deal with citizens who exhibit those behaviors.

6. Create a commercial encouraging other to join your society. In this commercial, explain leisure activities, educational systems, the town layout, job opportunities, etc. Tell people why they would want to live here. This commercial may be filmed and uploaded to YouTube to be shown to class OR performed as a skit (with props) live.

Finally, you and your partners will professionally present your society to the rest of the class. You will dress professionally and explain all of the above aspects to the rest of the class.

Here is the rubric that went along with the assignment.

Multimedia Project : Create Your Own Transcendentalist Society

Teacher Name: **Mr. Provenzano**

Students Names: _____ _____

CATEGORY	20	15	10	5
Presentation	Well-rehearsed with smooth delivery that holds audience attention.	Rehearsed with fairly smooth delivery that holds audience attention most of the time.	Delivery not smooth, but able to maintain interest of the audience most of the time.	Delivery not smooth and audience attention often lost.
Organization	Content is well organized using headings or bulleted lists to group related material.	Uses headings or bulleted lists to organize, but the overall organization of topics appears flawed.	Content is logically organized for the most part.	There was no clear or logical organizational structure, just lots of facts.
Attractiveness	Makes excellent use of font, color, graphics, effects, etc. to enhance the presentation.	Makes good use of font, color, graphics, effects, etc. to enhance to presentation.	Makes use of font, color, graphics, effects, etc. but occasionally these detract from the	Use of font, color, graphics, effects etc. but these distract from the presentaion content.

Content (X2)	Covers topic in-depth with details and examples. Subject knowledge is excellent.	Includes essential knowledge about the topic. Subject knowledge appears to be good.	Includes essential information about the topic but there are 1-2 factual errors.	Content is minimal OR there are several factual errors.
Mechanics	No misspellings or grammatical errors.	Three or fewer misspellings and/or mechanical errors.	Four misspellings and/or grammatical errors.	More than 4 errors in spelling or grammar.
Originality	Product shows a large amount of original thought. Ideas are creative and inventive.	Product shows some original thought. Work shows new ideas and insights.	Uses other people\'s ideas (giving them credit), but there is little evidence of original thinking.	Uses other people\'s ideas, but does not give them credit.
Requirements	All requirements are met and exceeded.	More than one requirement was not completely met.	More than two requirements were not completely met.	Many requirements were not completely met.

This project still has flaws, but I hope it shows the evolution of projects over time. The point totals are still all over the place, and the things that are being assessed are not equally weighted based on student understanding, but the rubric does allow for more feedback and room for comments.

Another aspect of this project that is pretty crazy is that it was designed to be very flawed. One of the main parts of the transcendentalist unit was having students explore identity and individuality. This project was designed to test students to see if they would follow all of the directions as they were laid out or work to create something different and meaningful that demonstrated their understanding of transcendentalist beliefs.

I gave this project to students for several years, and there was about one group per year that risked their grade and did something different. It was always a great discussion with the students about following directions, being an individual, and showing how societies really worked. The groups that did their own thing would create their own rubric and directions and present why they think the assignment was a bad one and not aligned with the true principles of transcendentalism.

Final Thoughts on Recipe Projects

Recipe projects are a fine place to start if you are nervous about giving up control of assignments to students. Sometimes, a recipe project is a good way for a teacher to start the year to get a sense of what the students are capable of before opening up future projects and allowing students to create meaning and demonstrate understanding. It is not the type of project that should be given to students all year. As teachers, we need to push ourselves to grow beyond the traditional types of lessons. I did not have access to the amount of information that is available today when I started. I would have loved to have access to teachers from all over the world to see how they do things. Do not fall into the trap of doing the same thing over and over again because it is easy. Teaching is hard, but that is what makes great lessons and projects feel so good at the end of the day.

"Do not fall into the trap of doing the same thing over and over again because it is easy."

Teacher Reflection

Do you have an example of one of your own lessons that would be considered a recipe lesson? Share it here with some ideas on how you can change it to give students more options.

CHAPTER

3

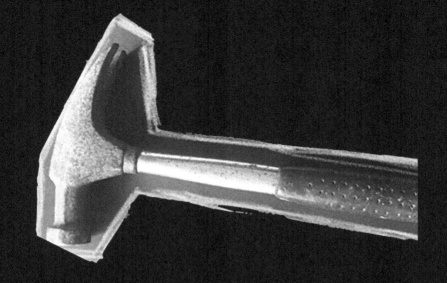

THE
ALL-CLASS
PROJECT

All-class projects are large in scope and tend to be outlined by the teacher. A small group of students could not accomplish an all-class project. Also, this is a great project type to encourage collaboration. The all-class project can be approached in two ways:

Option A

Students are broken up into smaller groups to complete a part of the project. Then, they come together with their individual parts to have a completed project. Think *Voltron* or *Mighty Morphin Power Rangers*. The groups do not need to communicate with one another to complete their smaller projects before they are brought together to create the final product.

The types of projects that the smaller groups work on can be recipe projects or completely student-driven projects. It is all dependent on what the final artifact is going to be at the end of the project.

Student Symbolism Exhibit

As part of reading a novel in class, having students explore symbols, and their meanings is an important part of the experience. Once students have a firm grasp of the symbols in the story, a large class project can be created that has students work in groups to create their own symbolic art installation that will symbolize an aspect of the book. They can use whatever medium they want to create their symbolic display, and everyone will come together, in the end, to host an event to showcase the art.

Students work in smaller groups with specific symbols to explore and have the freedom to create projects of their own design based on something they want to be represented through a symbol.

Option B

The second type of all-class project has the students working in smaller groups, but collaboration and coordination are crucial in creating the final artifact at the end. This type of project can be very tricky and really requires a teacher to have a solid understanding of how their class interacts for this to work. These types of projects require tons of planning on the teacher's end before the project begins and that teacher is active in and out of class to make sure everything comes together for the final presentation. This is a time consuming, but very rewarding, project type.

The Epic Romeo and Juliet Project

This is the most intensive and complex lesson I have ever created, and it is one of my absolute favorites. The entire lesson is very long and complex, but I will summarize here and provide a link for the full lesson download.

I had always struggled with teaching *Romeo and Juliet* to my grade 9 students. I dreaded it because I could not find the best way to engage the students in the reading. I was stuck in the "make the kids stand and read to one another" awkward Shakespeare trope. I needed to change things up, so I decided to have my students create their own version of *Romeo and Juliet*.

I decided it would be cool if we collaborated on this project with students from another school in another state. We divided up the acts of the play and set up the project like this:

- There would be actors, writers, directors, film crew, costumes, and a soundtrack.
- Each class would be assigned a specific act of *Romeo and Juliet*.
- Students that wanted to play parts in the production would audition for their parts.
- Students would write down what job they would like to do for the production. They would have a first, second, and third choice.
- The writers would edit the play but keep Shakespeare's original language.
- Directors would work with all of the other groups to create the best situation for filming.
- The film crew worked with the director, and the costume department and soundtrack team worked with the writers to get a sense of tone for the different scenes.
- The teacher acted as the producer and helped students secure the video equipment and the on-campus shooting locations during and after school.

The main part of this entire project is that no matter what part a student had, they had to spend time with the text to understand what was happening in the story. They had to collaborate with students in other departments, other classes, and another school to make sure everything lined up correctly. There were so many great stories that came out of this project, but there was one story that really stands out to me.

A student came to me before school to talk about the project. She was on the script team. She liked to write but was not a fan of reading. She chose the script team in the hopes of writing something awesome.

"Mr. P., have you read *Romeo and Juliet* before?"

"Yes, I've been teaching it for ten years. I've read it many times."

"Ya, but do you know what Shakespeare was writing about?"

"Yup."

"So, you know all about the dirty jokes in the play?"

"Yes, Shakespeare wrote some pretty dirty jokes for the time."

"Not just for the time. They are super dirty. I was reading some of the lines for the play, and I was trying to figure out what some of the things meant, and I was blown away. I then found out that he used puns to hide the meaning of what he was saying so he wouldn't get in trouble for being gross."

"Ya, his use of puns is pretty well known. I'm glad you looked that up."

"So, I just wanted to be clear that we will not get in trouble for keeping those lines in there. I don't think Romeo should say some of these things, but I guess we could keep them in there, and if anyone asks, we could give them the non-dirty meaning just like Shakespeare did."

"You are the writer. I trust you to make the right decision."

"Thanks, Mr. P. Forget I stopped by." Walking away, she said, "I can't believe the school lets us read this."

This conversation made me so happy because I had a student doing a close reading of the play, research for further understanding, and then coming to the realization of what Shakespeare was doing with his double entendres and deciding to do the same thing. I could have never accomplished this with a stand and read approach.

In the end, this project was a smashing success. The students created a 90-minute movie about two rival private schools and the star-crossed lovers that attended them. We had a joint premiere on a Saturday morning in our school auditoriums. Every student received a hard copy on DVD, and it is something students still talk about when I see them. It was one of the most stressful lessons I have ever done, but it might be the best.

Here is how the work is divided up for the whole class project approach.

Students	Teachers
Have some freedom to create and design their project based on the teacher's directions. Have input on what the final product looks like. Are self-motivated to complete the project. Are allowed self-expression. Are encouraged to collaborate.	Give students some power to create within a set of guidelines. Do most of the work on the front end to set it up. Support students throughout the process. Need to consider student interactions and chemistry. Create a rubric that supports the different elements of the project.

Final Thoughts on All-Class Projects

One of the things I learned is that all-class projects are not for every class every year. The epic *Romeo and Juliet* project was the right project at the right time for the skill set of those students. I thought about doing it again, but the stars never aligned to make it possible, and that is ok. It forced me to adjust my projects, and it is good to tailor assignments to students every year. It keeps it fresh and allows for personalization for a greater chance of student success.

I also think that you need a few years under your belt before you try to engage an entire class or multiple classes like I did. I was able to do this based on several years of understanding how classes ran at my school, and I felt comfortable letting students have the freedom to take ownership of aspects of the project. You can read more about the epic *Romeo and Juliet* project on my website, and you can find the complete lesson plan here (https://bit.ly/2mBmJYm). Feel free to take it and alter it however you want.

Teacher Reflection

Do you have an epic project that you have always wanted to do with your students? What is it, and why haven't you done it?

CHAPTER

4

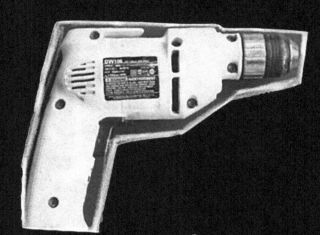

TOOL
SPECIFIC
PROJECT

This is a project on the PBL spectrum that drives the PBL purists nuts. They think that it can't be PBL if you dictate the tools that the students have to use to demonstrate an understanding of a concept. I would normally totally agree with this, but there are times that the teacher wants to expose students to a particular tool, and the best way to do that is through a project. Not all tools need to be centered around a project. I wouldn't build an entire project around using Google Slides. I think there is something to be said for teaching students how to make engaging presentations, but an entire project dedicated to that is a bit much. If a student wants to use Slides as part of their project, that would be a good time for some support on the side from the teacher for that particular project.

Sometimes, the teacher wants to introduce a tool to the classroom because it can open up many more project ideas for different students who have never used it before, or the teacher wants to have the class use the tool because they know it will be engaging for a part of the class that is in need of some attention.

This type of project, like the other projects, can be bad if it is the only type of project that is ever assigned by the teacher. Like most things in life, too much of one thing can be very bad. All things in moderation. Here is how a tool-based project is set up.

Students	Teachers
Do not have a say in the tools used to demonstrate understanding. Need to rely on teacher support when stuck or confused. Have little say on the parameters of the project. May have some freedom on how the tool is used, depending on the tool.	Choose the tool and the requirements of the project. Support students throughout the use of the tool as students become acquainted with how it works. Need to have a strong understanding of how the tool works if they expect the students to power through speed bumps. May give students some freedom on how the tool is used, depending on what the tool is.

Interactive Fiction with Python Code

I have spent the past few years exploring Python code through my use of the Raspberry Pi computer. Python is a text-based coding language that can be used to code lights, sensors, cameras, and even games.

I found this tutorial online created by Raspberry Pi that showed users how to create a text-based computer game. A text-based computer game is one of the very first types of games ever created on computers. The player types in the commands for the game, and the game types out the response. Zork is one of the most famous text-based games ever made. Text-based games are actually called Interactive Fiction, and after going through the tutorial and creating my own game (https://bit.ly/2IFESE7), I thought this would be the perfect project for sixth graders' creative writing unit. I connected with the sixth-grade English teacher, explained to her the plan, and she was pumped. Here is the outline of the lesson.

Step 1:

Work with students to understand the elements of a story. Start by reading some stories that have a Gothic tone to them. Adventure short stories are also really good for this project. The Monkey's Paw, The Most Dangerous Game, The Yellow Wallpaper, and A Rose for Emily are just a few off the top of my head. Focus on plot, protagonist, antagonist, and story endings.

Step 2:

Introduce students to the Raspberry Pi RPG tutorial (https://bit.ly/2UlqPjN). Work with students to complete the tutorial over the next two to three days. Insist that students complete the tutorial in full before altering it for their own game. This is to ensure that they understand how everything works before changing things. Here are some tips to make this part of the lesson run smoothly.

- Make sure students create an account using Trinket (the web app they are using to write the code), so they can save their work and prevent the loss of code.
- The most common mistakes that students are going to make are missing commas, quotation marks, and incorrect indentation.
- When in doubt, refer to the code on the Raspberry Pi tutorial to make sure everything looks the way it is supposed to.
- It is always good to have multiple sets of eyes trying to debug an issue with code. There were plenty of times I could not find the error, and then another student found it right away. Our eyes can be deceiving. The more eyes, the better.

Step 3:

Have students start to develop their own story that can be used as the groundwork for a game. Have students focus on their protagonist, antagonist, overall plot, items, and ending. This can be in an outline, or it can be a fully developed story. Some students will want to write a full narrative, and others might prefer the outline. It is important to note that their story does not have to take place in a house. The "rooms" they will be coding for their game can be rooms in a dungeon or spaces in a cave. They could be planets that their space captain travels to, or each doorway could be a portal to another dimension. Don't let students get stuck on the idea that they have to build a story and game around a house.

Step 4:

Students need to draw out their map. The more complex the story, the more complex the map will need to be so the students can accurately code the game. How many rooms a student wants to add is up to the teacher or student. I would suggest having at least six to ten rooms to make it a semi-challenging game. Students will want to make their game tough and generally will not need to be prodded into adding multiple rooms, monsters, items, etc.

Step 5:

Students should spend the next couple of class periods working on the code to create their game. They will add details to the rooms and create a wonderful backstory to their game that will make it more engaging. You can use my code (https://bit.ly/31LWEFt) as a starting point to create a more complex narrative.

Step 6:

When all of the students have completed the code, have them share their game with others, and take a class period playing student games. Kids love playing their games and showcasing the work they did.

Extensions:

Here are some things you can add to this lesson to really have the students dive deep into the work.

- Have students create a commercial advertising their game. This can be a video or audio commercial.
- Have students create cover art for their game in the style of old school computer games.

- If you have students create a commercial and cover art, consider having them create a website that would host the story, game, commercial, and cover art. Adobe Spark is an awesome tool because it can help you accomplish all of the above—and it's free!
- Consider allowing students to form groups that will become their own gaming company. A student will be in charge of the code, another student will be in charge of the story, and another student will be in charge of the marketing.

Assessment

We did not do a formal assessment with this project. This was an in-class assignment and is designed to strengthen students' writing and reading skills. Some of the bonus skills that are supported with this project are spatial reasoning, critical thinking, computational thinking, design, and other concepts that go beyond the typical ELA assignment. If a teacher wanted to create an assessment rubric for this assignment, they could, but I feel that it takes away the joy of the work.

As a teacher thinks about creating a tool-specific project, lots of thought needs to go into the "why" of choosing a specific tool.

- Is the tool going to be something that students will use again?
- Does it make the project special or stand out in a way that would not be possible without it?
- Will the students learn other skills while using the tool for the project?
- Does learning the new tool cause more stress than needed for the lesson?

- Are students ready to tackle a new tool at this point in the school year?

Spend time going over the tool and asking those questions because there is nothing worse than choosing a tool that blows up in students' faces. That is the fastest way to destroy a lesson and tool for students.

Tool-Specific Project Final Thoughts

I love the idea of doing things differently and having some fun with a specific tool that challenges students to think a little differently and create something outside of the norm for them. It is so important for teachers to explore different tools and see how they might be used in the classroom. It is also ok to not be a certified expert in the tool, but you should have some basic understanding of how it is used and have YouTube tutorials bookmarked on your computer ready to share with your students. As long as you are honest about not knowing everything about the tool with students, they are far more understanding and will work with you and other students to troubleshoot any issues that come up. Used occasionally, the tool-specific project has the chance to open up student creativity and support a wide variety of learners in any classroom.

Teacher Reflection

Do you have any tools that you would love to introduce to your students? What are they, and why do you think students should use them for a project?

CHAPTER

5

OPEN
PROJECT-BASED
LEARNING
WITH
TEACHER
OBJECTIVES

We are getting closer to the purest form of PBL. Open PBL with Teacher Objectives (OPBLTO) is a fairly simple form of PBL, but it requires the teacher to truly entrust the students with making all of the decisions regarding the project. Here is what it looks like for the student and the teacher.

Students	Teachers
Chooses a medium based on their specific skill set that allows them to fully demonstrate their understanding of the material covered in class. Work with the teacher during the project to make sure they are meeting the objectives outlined by the teacher. Create a rubric with the teacher to allow for an accurate assessment of their project when it is done. Take on the responsibility of the different aspects that make up the project.	Give a broad project assignment to the student to demonstrate an understanding of a specific aspect of the curriculum covered in class. Support the students during the project time and is very active during the class periods. Help students create a rubric for their projects to accurately assess their work. Hand a large amount of power over to the students by trusting them to use a medium for the project that suits their skill set.

OPBLTO is the biggest leap a teacher makes on their PBL journey. The teacher moves away from choosing the tools and only provides a broad topic for students to address. This allows the student to take full responsibility, with teacher guidance, in demonstrating an understanding of a concept to the teacher and the class. Here is a brief example of what it might look like in my ELA class.

A General Example

After reading a novel in class and discussing it over a couple of weeks, an OPBLTO assignment would look like this.

We have read _____ and discussed it over the past couple of weeks. Demonstrate your understanding of theme, symbolism, motif, and characterization. You have one week to create a project that demonstrates your understanding of all of these aspects of the story.

This format works for any story read at any time. You can just fill in a new book for every project. For me, I would not get to the OPBLTO type of projects until the start of the second semester because I needed to gradually work students toward the freedom of owning their projects. Just starting off the year with this would lead to lots of confusion. Unless you are at a school that regularly allows students to choose the way they want to demonstrate understanding, gradually getting students there with different, smaller projects, is the most effective way I have found to integrate PBL into the classroom.

This approach to PBL is scary because the teacher has to trust the students to create a project that will fully demonstrate their understanding of the topics covered in class. This trust comes from time together in the classroom. This type of project is going to vary from class to class and year to year. I have had some classes where students were ready after the first eight weeks, and others needed another eight weeks to get there. The beauty of PBL is that it allows for differentiation across the board.

Over the years, I have received the very best projects when I moved to OPBLTO. The format for the assignment is always the same, and I have used it for different classes, age groups, and stories. Here are two examples that are worth sharing.

Glimpse of Gothic Art

One of the units in my American literature class was Gothic literature. We would read Poe, Hawthorne, and others and explore the dark side of American literature. As part of this unit, we discussed the different elements that made up a Gothic piece of literature. For their project, I asked them to demonstrate an understanding of the Gothic elements. I received some great projects from students over the years, but one has stood the test of time for me, and I'm so happy I get to share them with you here. Take a look at these photos from my student Nicole Sceglio.

These are just a few of the pictures that Nicole took and presented to the class. She placed her images on some Google Slides and talked about the process. I remember watching each slide pull up and knowing exactly what Gothic element she was going to talk about. Students felt the same and told her so when she was done. Students were blown away and a little freaked out by the photos. She didn't even take a photography class at school. These were amazing photos, and her friends encouraged her to sign up for photography the next year. She was so excited when I asked her permission to showcase her photos for this book.

What I love about this project example is that it is exactly why students should be given the opportunity to demonstrate an understanding of a concept in ways that are meaningful to them. She created these beautiful works of art while exploring the elements of Gothic literature.

These are photos that students still talk about, and I always think about when reading any type of Gothic work. That is exactly what is supposed to happen with a truly great project. Showcasing her work in class gave her the courage to sign up for photo classes and explore this side of her that she thought was just a silly hobby. Giving students a chance to shine on center stage with their creations is always an awesome thing to make happen in the classroom. Those instances increase exponentially when PBL is brought into the classroom.

Gatsby Rap Battle

My second example revolved around The *Great Gatsby*. I gave students the task of demonstrating an understanding of the theme, symbolism, and characterization in the story. A group of students decided to come together and create an amazing rap song all about the book. Sebastian, the leader of the group, created the beats for the song, and each member of the four-person group took a character (Gatsby, Tom, Daisy, and Nick) and crafted lyrics for the song that would address the objectives. You have to listen to fully appreciate it. Here is a link to the YouTube video. https://bit.ly/30LvcXl

> Nick- Boy from
> Massachusetts you already
> know. I'm about to go off on
> you with my incredulous flow
>
> Gatsby- My name is Jay
> Gatsby everybody knows,
> making money stalking Daisy
> that's just how it goes.
>
> Tom- Tom here to devour I'm
> the man of the hour I win all
> the women over with my
> money and power
>
> Daisy- Daisy Buchanan I'm
> going off like a cannon, I'm
> rich and own a whole lot I
> know you want what I got.

I was not sure how this project was going to end up when they were done. They assured me they were going to create something epic. I had to remind myself that I need to trust my students. One of the students, the voice of Gatsby, created the music for the rap and shared it with other students to create their lyrics. They were all able to individually create their work, and "Gatsby" edited it all together. It was a wonderful technical feat.

If you listen to the lyrics, they are simply amazing. It shows a depth and understanding of the text that a multiple-choice test could never truly assess. This went above and beyond the assignment to explore a theme, a few symbols, and a recurring motif.

There are a few reasons that this project stands out to me as a wonderful example of OPBLTO.

- The openness of the project let these students really push themselves creatively. Two of the four students would not be considered poets, and one of them spoke more in this rap project than they did in class all year.

- The part where Daisy starts her rap is epic. The girl that did her part was in the school's show choir, but she never had to write lyrics and match this type of beat before. When her part dropped, the class went crazy!

- Sebastian is an aspiring music creator, and this was a chance for him to showcase his music skills. I know the positive feedback for him really impacted him in a great way.

- Student engagement after the song was played was amazing! The students dove into the lyrics and were discussing the meaning of the song in relation to the book. Students were doing a class analytical read of a song to connect to the close reading they did of a novel. That is nuts!

I could provide hundreds of examples of student work for this type of project. In one year, I could have three sections on American literature with about 30 students in the class. For one assigned open project, I could get around 80–90 different projects. Every year, I would receive brand new projects that would inspire me and impact everyone in the classroom. That is something I really want ELA teachers to think about. Projects are not just about assessing students understanding, they can impact student learning in the class because others are engaging in the projects that students have created and are now sharing with the class.

Assessing Open Projects with Teacher Objectives

Assessing these types of projects tend to terrify teachers. With 30 different projects, how can you create a rubric that covers a movie, a puppet show, a graphic novel, and so much more? This was my concern as well when I started using these types of projects in the classroom. At first, I was trying to create individual rubrics for each student and their project. This was a logistical nightmare. I then realized that I could create broad rubrics like I created a broad assignment. Here is an example of a broad rubric I created for a project.

Teacher Name: **Mr. Provenzano**

Student Name: _____

CATEGORY	20	17	15	12
Presentation	Well-rehearsed with smooth delivery that holds audience attention.	Rehearsed with fairly smooth delivery that holds audience attention most of the time.	Delivery not smooth, but able to maintain interest of the audience most of the time.	Delivery not smooth and audience attention often lost.
-	Covers topic in-depth with details and examples. Subject knowledge is excellent.	Includes essential knowledge about the topic. Subject knowledge appears to be good.	Includes essential information about the topic but there are 1-2 factual errors.	Content is minimal OR there are several factual errors.
-	Covers topic in-depth with details and examples. Subject knowledge is excellent.	Includes essential knowledge about the topic. Subject knowledge appears to be good.	Includes essential information about the topic but there are 1-2 factual errors.	Content is minimal OR there are several factual errors.
-	Covers topic in-depth with details and examples. Subject knowledge is excellent.	Includes essential knowledge about the topic. Subject knowledge appears to be good.	Includes essential information about the topic but there are 1-2 factual errors.	Content is minimal OR there are several factual errors.
Originality	Product shows a large amount of original thought. Ideas are creative and inventive.	Product shows some original thought. Work shows new ideas and insights.	Uses other people\'s ideas (giving them credit), but there is little evidence of original thinking.	Uses other people\'s ideas, but does not give them credit.

Notice that I left the three middle content areas blank. I can print one of these sheets off and write in the areas that the students need to focus on for their project. Traditionally, I have theme and symbolism as pretty standard parts of analysis, but sometimes I like to have characterization, motif, or other literary items in those spots, depending on where the conversation went in class. Once I added the elements I wanted the students to focus on for the project, I would make copies and give them to the students.

The presentation part of the rubric is pretty standard for me because I believe that students need to work on their presentation skills. Standing and speaking in front of people is an important skill. This part is easily adjusted for students with anxiety issues. Depending on the student, they can present before school. They have the option of bringing a friend or having another teacher in the room. I encourage those students to slowly build their audience over time with the hope they can do a full class presentation by the end of the school year. Some get there and others don't, but there is always growth, and that is what matters most.

I also have originality on the rubric because I want the students to understand that creating something new and original is powerful, and if they are inspired by other work, they need to cite that information and give credit to those people. This part of the rubric has led to some great conversations regarding inspiration for work and how to properly attribute that influence in a piece that is presented in class. These are some of the bonus lessons that come with doing PBL in the classroom.

Student-Created Rubrics

One of the other approaches to assessing OPBLTO is to let students create their own rubric. This is something I have found that works well at the high school level but could work at the middle school level with more guidance. Having students create the rubric offers them more control of the project and helps them see what is valued in their work to them and to the audience. There is also a boost in ownership when the student accepts the responsibility of creating the assessment tool for their project. The thought is, If I can't pass a project that I came up with and wrote the rubric for, what the heck am I doing?

Guiding students to create rubrics is a great way to explore assessment with students and have them see a bit of what teachers are doing when they create assignments. I share with them the tools I use, RubiStar (https://bit.ly/1s6K4Lk), and we work on building a rubric together. We discuss point values, important elements of a project, and what they want to be assessed for their work. Getting students to understand assessment is important because it will guide them on future projects and assignments down the line.

Final Thoughts on Open Project-Based Learning with Teacher Objectives

Bringing this type of project to my classroom changed everything I thought I knew about education. There was this fear in moving to more open projects that allowed for more student choice, but I needed to move beyond that fear and trust that I have prepared students to be able to make these decisions, and I needed to be prepared to support them when they stumbled.

Another fear I had was that my students were not going to perform well on the standardized final exam for each semester. I was so nervous about the end of the semester grades because my changes could negatively impact the students and their overall grades that impact GPA and potentially their college of choice. It was crazy. When the dust settled, my students did just as well and, in some cases, even better than students who were not involved in a PBL environment like the one I created in the classroom. That would hold true for all of my classes moving forward. I would argue that if the results are the same, what reasons are there to not try to implement a PBL environment in the classroom?

Teacher Reflection

Where do you think an open project would fit in your curriculum? How might students react to the freedom of choosing their own medium for their project?

CHAPTER

6

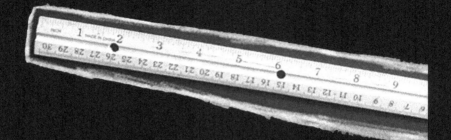

Cumulative Projects

Another type of project that can be used in the class-room is the cumulative project. These projects are much broader in scope than other projects because the students are being asked to take a wider view of a particular question. While a traditional project will ask students to focus on the content that was covered in class, the cumulative project asks students to take a look at a large portion of the curriculum. This might be a marking period or an entire semester. The goal of the cumulative project is to get students to think about the connections that can be made over a set time of the year. One of the goals of a middle school or high school ELA class is to get students to see the over-riding theme that connects everything that is covered in the class or to ask students to go the extra mile and see how what has been covered in class relates to the world around them or even them specifically.

Cumulative projects tend to be structured like OPBLTO projects, but they can be set up to have students explore a specific connection the teacher dictates, or the teacher allows the students to find the connections and works to make those connections clear through the course of a presentation. No matter who chooses the connection, the students must be given time and support to explore these connections over that set period. At least one week of class time should be given to allow students to do the research and create the project needed to address a question that covers so much ground. Here are what the students and teachers are responsible for in a cumulative project.

Students	Teachers
Identify the common theme or motif over the designated part of the curriculum.	Provide students with the parts of the curriculum that will be covered.
Research and support the claim that addresses the connection.	Support student research on the curriculum.
Choose a medium that will allow them to demonstrate an understanding of the texts and their connections.	Conference with students on their project to support their work.
Create a rubric to assess their ability to demonstrate an understanding of the content.	Support student creation of a rubric.

Setting Up a Cumulative Project

Setting up a project of this scope requires serious planning on the teacher's part. I've put together some steps to help guide you through the creation of your cumulative project.

Step 1: Create Your Timeline
You need to have a clear timeline of when you want the students to start on the project and present. This has to happen at the end of the marking period, so you must schedule this time correctly. You do not want to run out of time because that will be reflected in the quality of the work

students submit. Give yourself some wiggle room, but try very hard to stick to the timeline you create.

Step 2:

Identify some of the themes, motifs, symbols, etc., that connect your course. These items will be the driving force of the project, and you will want to note them in advance and bring them to the attention of your students during the course. These conversations will be the heart of the research students will do to connect stories, poems, and other pieces.

Step 3:

Decide on the framework for the project and assign it early. If you want the students to focus on themes or symbols, that decision needs to be made early so you can create the assignment sheet and give it to the students with enough time for them to digest it and get to work. I do not recommend giving the assignment to students at the start of the week to work on the project. Try and give it to them at least one week before the start of the project. The more of a head start a student can have on their research, the better the project will be for everyone.

Step 4:

Create a rubric template that students can use or alter for their project. This will save some students the stress of the assessment part of the project. They might take exactly what you created, or they might take parts and adjust it based on their particular medium.

Step 5:

Be available. This is big because you are going to en-counter students that have no idea where to start and will get very anxious. You will know who those students are, and you want to make sure you are prepared to guide them along in the project. That guidance will help them be suc-cessful and calm the nerves of those students. Try and make time before and after school to conference with stu-dents as needed.

By taking these five steps, you will be able to create an amazing cumulative project that will truly allow students to demonstrate an understanding over a much larger part of the curriculum. To me, it is something I would like to see replace all final semester exams.

Interpretive Dance for the Win

One of my standard bad teacher jokes involved listing all of the different types of projects students could do for a particular assignment.

"For this project, you could do a puppet show, paint-ing, movie, graphic novel, sketch comedy, or even interpretive dance."

Students would always laugh, and a few boys would sometimes say they were going to do it, but they never did. I was always left a little disappointed each year that nobody wanted to dance for class. One year, two students did not disappoint me at all.

After doing my traditional spiel on types of projects, two ladies came up to me and said they wanted to do the interpretive dance. These were two of my absolute bright-est students in the class, and they were both in the choir, so I knew they were not messing with me. They asked what the requirements would be for that type of project, and I just stared at them blankly. I never thought about the requirements because nobody had ever expressed interest, and I do not know anything about dance. I said I trusted them to make it as complex as they needed as long as they were able to demonstrate an understanding of how themes and symbols connected the novels we covered in the second semester. They smiled and said they could do it. What they submitted is one of my all-time favorite student projects. It gives me chills every time I show it at a conference in a session or a keynote. (https://bit.ly/2AN3BtX)

This is one of those projects I feel that only ELA teachers can truly appreciate. I had a feeling this project was going to be amazing, so I gave the girls a couple of extra days by having them present last. That extra time paid off, and they created something simply beautiful. They created art to express an understanding of complex themes and symbols in two pieces of American literature. They listened to 100 songs to find the right ones to pair with their assessment of the characters they chose from *The Great Gatsby* and *The Catcher in the Rye*. I had never heard of "Hurricane Drunk" before, but it is the perfect song for Holden Caulfield. The project received a standing ovation from students in the class, and a common comment from students was, "I don't know anything about dance, but I know everything you did in that dance, and it totally makes sense."

That is the fundamental point of doing projects—to demonstrate an understanding of a specific topic in a way that others can see. The students had created a rubric for this assignment, and I could not bring myself to mark it up. Their creation was so well done, a rubric would be an injustice. I simply gave them full credit and talked with the students after. The songs and dance moves might not mean anything to people outside of the class or ELA, but that is not the purpose of the assessment. Without a doubt, I can watch that dance and know that they understood the connections they displayed.

To be able to complete this dance, the students had to spend hours going over songs, finding symbols that would represent the characters, make sure those symbols made sense in the context of a dance, and then choreograph four different dances for each song and connection they made. How anyone could suggest that those students did not have a strong understanding of the connections between those two novels is beyond me.

"They created something beautiful in a world made ugly by standardized testing."

They created something beautiful in a world made ugly by standardized testing. It's my favorite example to share with anyone interested in PBL, and I'm happy I get to share it here with all of you.

Final Thoughts on Cumulative Projects

Cumulative projects require lots of work on the front end by the teacher, support during the project, and dedicated time for students to create something amazing. It is not an easy type of project to do in a class, especially if you are new to PBL. It is something worth exploring after a year or two of integrating PBL into your class. I guarantee that students will enjoy demonstrating their understanding of the material covered in class over a semester ending multiple choice test or essay.

Teacher Reflection

What common thread do you have in your class that connects the material you cover in the curriculum? How might a project look at the end of a marking period or semester?

CHAPTER

7

GENIUS HOUR AND 20 TIME

One of the things that people say about the previous types of projects is that the students have some choice, but they are still confined to the content covered in class, so it is not the truest form of PBL. After I internally roll my eyes at the fact that those people love to spend their time tearing things down instead of recognizing positive student growth, I point them to Genius Hour/20 Time.

Let me explain the two names for the project to help clarify what I am talking about. Genius Hour and 20 Time are the same things with different names. How you implement them will determine what they are called.

Genius Hour

In Genius Hour, students are given an hour during the day to work on an independently chosen project. The students will research their topic and share what they learned in a presentation to the class. The dedicated time each day is referred to as Genius Hour. This tends to work best for elementary classes because the teachers have the flexibility to move the hour around during any given week.

20 Time

20 Time is a little different from Genius Hour because of the timing. In middle school and high school, schedules are not as flexible, and teachers tend to only see students once a day for 45–50 minutes. Instead of giving students time each day, the teacher gives the students one day of the week (20%) to work on their independent project. 20 Time is the one day of the week of independent work in class.

The objectives of both are the same, but the timing is a bit different, so there are different names. I will stick to using 20 Time because that is what I used as a high school teacher implementing it in my classroom.

Implementation

Implementing 20 Time can be a bit scary and seem impossible. It can be set up to work for a marking period (8 weeks), a full semester (16 weeks), or a full year (32 weeks). The teacher has the discretion to decide how long students are going to work on their project. The more time you give the students, the larger the project they can tackle. Keep that in mind as you decide on the length of 20 Time. Since I always jump in with both feet, I wanted to try a full year of 20 Time.

I thought there would be no way for me to carve out 20% of my curriculum to allow time for students to work on their own project one day a week. There are about 32 weeks in a school year. If I wanted to give students one day a week, that is a little over a month worth of instructional time. Out of pure curiosity, I spent a couple of weeks in the summer looking at my curriculum with the intent on cutting as much as I could to see how close I could get. I was surprised at what I found.

When I was finished, I was able to cut 35 days out of my curriculum. I was blown away by this. It was not as tough as I thought it would be, but I still had to make some tough choices. Here is how I went about it.

- I cut (almost) all films shown in class. I kept *Dead Poets Society* because it is just too good to cut, and it was different from the other films because it was not just a movie version of something we read.
- I shortened the amount of time I gave students on different projects by a day here and there. This was

tough, but I thought about the projects and found that the students could do them in a slightly shortened time frame.

- I tossed some lessons that I had been doing for years because I loved them, but, when I was honest with myself, were ultimately redundant. I covered the material in other places in a better way, so those lessons did not need to be there.
- The last thing I did was condense some of the reading for certain texts. I increased the amount that needed to be read each night by a little for each text, and that opened up days at the end of the year.

Now that I had the time, I needed to find a structure to support the use of that time. I needed to make sure I had a system that would support students as they explored different topics across a varied spectrum. I came up with my guidelines for 20 Time.

1. Every Friday will be designated for 20 Time.

No matter what happens, Friday is the day that the students have 20 Time. It needs to be a sacred day for the students. As a teacher, you will feel compelled to adjust the schedule and "borrow" a day from 20 Time, but you can't do it. The minute you take a day away from the students, you invalidate the work they are doing. If their work is truly important, you won't take their time away from it.

I chose Friday because it seemed like a logical way to end a week. After the first year of 20 Time in the classroom, I asked students about moving 20 Time to another day, and their feedback supported a Friday choice. Any other day would break up the learning of the content, and nobody wants to work on their project on Monday. Pick whatever day works best for you, but I suggest Friday.

2. Choose a topic that is new and interesting to you.

Choosing a project for 20 Time is one of the hardest parts for students. I've had some very stressed students come to me for support on choosing a topic because they have never been given the freedom to explore something they are interested in learning more about. As the teacher, you need to work with students and help them find that one thing that can drive them throughout the period you chose. I tell kids, "Go big or go home," because they will not get another opportunity to do something like this again.

20 Time is only discussed and worked on during Friday class time, so that is only three to four class meetings. Some students will know what they want to do right away and will begin their research. Others will take some time and need multiple meetings with the teacher. Be patient and listen. Every student has something they can spend time exploring but just need some help getting there.

3. Produce a product or achieve a goal.

Students need something tangible to work toward. A goal in which they are actively working to produce something allows them to focus their work. For me, a full school year is a long time for students to be focused on researching their topic. Their goal allows me to help redirect them if they get stuck. "What is the next step toward meeting your goal?" or "How is what you're doing moving you toward your goal?" are just a couple of questions I can use while checking in with students to assess where they are in their project.

4. Complete the information sheet.

20 Time Project Information Sheet

Last Name:_____ First Name:_____Period:_____

Twitter (Optional):_____ Instagram (Optional):_____

Blog Address:_____.blogspot.com

Project Title:_____

Project Description:
_____
_____
_____
_____
_____
_____

This sheet is given to students, and they fill it out when they are ready to confirm their final project. I make a copy and give the original back to the students. This is a great way to keep students focused on exactly what their project is and allows me to have quick access to student projects as well. I was doing this with three classes of 30, and I needed a reference guide to keep track of everything.

5. Choose a mentor.
While teachers wear many hats over any school year, they can't be a mentor to every student for every project. The mentor needs to be the first line of help when the

student is stuck. It can be a different teacher, a family member, or even a friend if they are an expert in the area they are exploring. That said, I did serve as a mentor to some students who focused on writing projects. A student wanted to write and publish a book of poetry, so I helped her with her writing. Not all students needed to rely on their mentor heavily, but some worked hand in hand with their mentor. Parents loved this aspect because it had students connecting with family members for their projects.

6. Reflect on their work.

Reflection is so important to all learners. For this project, I wanted students to think back on the work they did over the year. I had students write a blog post once a week for the first semester and then, based on their feedback, twice a month in the second semester. These blog posts were not graded and were designed to be informal. I made all of the links to the blogs accessible on Google Classroom so the students could read the updates of their peers. Some students expressed frustration at having to write, and others could not contain the awesomeness at what was going on in their project and would write more than was required.

The reading and writing of the blogs was a way to help support those skills over the school year. I was still teaching an ELA class, and I wanted to make sure that students were still reading and writing plenty over the year. Informal and ungraded writing still counts as writing. The blogs also come in handy for the final assessment of the 20 Time Project.

7. Share what you have learned.

Students are traditionally asked to share what they did in class, not what they learned. The question is designed to have students think about learning as something that happens based on what they did for their project. A student might have played three songs on the guitar, but he might have learned about sound or music creation throughout their project. The blog posts are a great reference point for students. Having that log to go back and see what their ups and downs were over a full school year adds some perspective they didn't have before.

8. Failure is an option.

This is very important for students to understand from the very beginning of the project. They are not being judged or graded on their ability to complete the project they chose. If they wanted to learn to juggle five balls, and they were only able to juggle four, that does not mean they have failed 20 Time. Students need to be encouraged to dream big and go for it. The fear of failing grades too often dictates the type of work that students will do in a class. Once the specter of failure is eliminated, students will try things never before dreamed by them.

These are not rules that are set in stone. Every teacher will adjust these guidelines to meet the needs of their students. The nicest part of 20 Time is that it can be implemented whenever the teacher wants for as long as they want. If the teacher wants to take it easy and start with one marking period to get a sense of how it goes, that is fine. If the teacher wants to dive in like I did and do it for a full year, that works as well. The teacher needs to feel comfortable taking on such a large project with the students. This is what the work looks like for students and teachers.

Students	Teachers
Choose a topic that is of interest and new to them.	Organize the days and times of Genius Hour/20 Time.
Find a mentor.	Provide guidance to students as they choose projects.
Reflect in writing regularly.	
	Be a mentor to a student project if needed.
Focus on what is learned, not just what is accomplished.	
	Read blogs and provide feedback.
Organize a speech and presentation.	
	Coach students on presentations.
Do not focus on failure.	

FAQ for 20 Time/Genius Hour

How do you assess student projects when they are all done?

As much as I would love to say you don't have to assess anything, I understand the realities that many teachers face when it comes to grading and report cards. We are not living in a gradeless society yet, but I hope we will in the near future.

I assess 20 Time in the following ways:

1. Blog Posts - When the students write the blog posts, they receive credit. It is a pass/fail sort of situation, but students only fail if they never do the post. I was flexible on due dates, and students got the work done in a timely manner. The beginning stages had them writing once a week and then it moved to every other week. I read them and left comments. I would mention grammar or content issues to them when we met in class, but I never used those mistakes to mark down their work. The blogs posts were not worth much in the way of points, but I wanted to recognize the work the students were doing as they reflected on their project.

2. Speech - At the end of the year, students have to give a six- to eight-minute talk on what they learned during their project. They can create slides and use any images to support their talk. I created a rubric and gave it to the students to give them a sense of how they were going to be assessed. I used TEDx Talks to model the type of speaking I'd like to see from my students. The students would give the speech in the auditorium in front of the entire class. Some exceptions were made for students with serious anxiety issues, but the vast majority spoke in the auditorium. The speech was weighted like an essay. It was a nice way to wrap up the project and have students work on their presentation skills.

3. Reflection - The very last piece of writing the students did for me was a reflection on the entire process of 20 Time. This served two purposes. The first is that it gave me feedback on the things that

worked and did not work from every student in my classes. The second allowed the students to spend time really thinking about the overall process and how it impacted them. Some of the comments moved me to tears because students said they felt so lucky to get to explore something they always wanted to learn, and it meant something for the school to support them. Some students said they liked 20 Time but were worried if doing this instead of traditional content would make them less prepared for their AP classes the next year. A few even said that it wasn't their thing, but it was nice to try out. As a teacher, you have to be ready to take feedback—the good and the bad—and work with it. The three to four comments that worried they were not prepared for the next school year really bothered me. It gave me such anxiety because I do not want to let anyone down. Luckily, my friends helped me focus on the 80 other reflections that were positive. Having students reflect on the process meant something to them and to me and allowed me to fine-tune the process for the next year.

Assessing 20 Time is really tough because the minute that students feel that their work could have a drastic impact on their grade, they start to play it safe or they don't play at all.

"The freedom from the specter of a grade hanging over them allows them to fully commit to their chosen project and fully embrace what is possible."

The freedom from the specter of a grade hanging over them allows them to fully commit to their chosen project and fully embrace what is possible. It is up to every teacher to find the best way to assess the students for this type of project.

How does 20 Time fit the curriculum?

Another very common question is about the curriculum. I think 20 Time is easiest to implement in ELA classes because it covers some of the most basic aspects of the course.

1. Research - Students spend a good deal of time researching their topic and finding out everything they need to know about it. The nice part of having students choose something new to them is that it pushes them to work on their research skills. No matter the topic, the students will be doing research. As the teacher, moving around the room, touching base with the students, and helping them with their research is an excellent way to use class time in the early stages of the project. I also connected with our media specialist to let her know that students might be coming down to the library to find books or other articles to support their research.

Research is such a fundamental skill for our students, and after doing 20 Time, I found that the students were more diligent in their research during this project than they were with my other assigned research projects. When students get to choose the topic, they are more engaged and will put in the effort that matters because the topic matters. You can't have 20 Time without research, and this core part of ELA classes is supported wonderfully here.

2. Writing - Students spend their time writing regular updates on their blogs and that practice, although informal, leads them to be better writers. The blog created a wonderful writing portfolio over an entire year. Students could go back and look at their posts from September and compare them with their posts from May and really see how far they have come in their writing. The students also felt far more comfortable with this informal approach to writing and allowed them to engage more fully. Even though it was not marked up as a formal piece of writing would be, the students grew to take more care of their writing knowing that parents and friends were also going to be reading their work. That expanded audience also helped to shape their writing.

Some students were able to sharpen their expository writing skills during 20 Time as well. They needed to write letters or emails to different businesses or adults asking for information or support, and they had never really done something like this. During those 20 Time days or when students stopped in to see me, I was able to help them format letters and work on being clear and concise when making requests. Sending these emails and letters were important to their project, so students took it far more seriously than writing letters to a fake business a teacher provided. This engagement is so important for the students to embrace the lessons learned while writing these types of letters.

The last part of the writing aspect of 20 Time is the formal reflection piece at the end of the year. The students were given the questions, "Do you think 20 Time was beneficial to your learning this year?" and "Should 20 Time continue as it is designed?" This is a fairly standard type of prompt for high school students to encounter. Take a position and support it with facts. I allowed for the first person in this essay since they were going to use personal examples, but, otherwise, it was a traditional writing assignment. By the end of the year, students had written plenty of formal papers, so this was a breeze compared to the others.

Throughout this entire project, students encountered many different forms of writing, and that is the cornerstone of any ELA class.

3. Reading and Proofreading - Students spend so much of their time reading during 20 Time—so

much that if I told them ahead of time that they would be doing lots of outside reading, many kids would have shut down. Since the reading was on things they were interested in learning about, it was never a problem. Some students focused on more nonfiction texts, and others needed more fiction. Since each student has a different project, their reading habits varied. It was nice to walk around and see the different types of books students were reading and how they would share them with other students when they were done. That wide variety of reading was an excellent addition to the curriculum I was required to cover in the class, and it gave students that freedom to choose what they wanted and needed to read and have those interests validated as part of a school project.

With all of the extra writing that students were doing, that meant there were more chances to proofread. This was not the case at the start of 20 Time, but as more and more people started to read their blog posts, they started to care more about potential spelling and grammar issues in their writing. Students would share their writing with others and help one another proofread for mistakes and content ideas. It was awesome to watch students do this on their own and learn from their mistakes. By using a blog, it was easy to show students the growth in their writing because they started to proofread.

As ELA teachers, we know that more reading and writing leads to better readers and writers. When the students are in charge of choosing the subject of the reading and the content of the writing, they will be more engaged and are more likely to grow in both of those areas.

4. Speaking/Presenting - While I believe that speaking and presenting are skills that should be explored in all content areas, the reality is that these concepts fall to the ELA teachers more often than not. Students knew from the very beginning of 20 Time that the project was going to end with a speech and presentation. We did not start talking about the specifics until about 45–60 days before it was time to present. The reason I waited because I wanted the students to focus on the content and not creating content for the presentation. I did tell them that the more effort they put into the reflections in the blog posts, the easier it would be to complete a presentation and speech. I also wait because the students will be doing presentations and speaking in class throughout the year, so they will get practice. It also allows me to see how the student might need support moving forward.

Some students were terrified to get in front of their classmates and share their learning, and others were happy to get up and share. As a teacher, like just about everything in the classroom, you know your kids, and you make the best judgment call for them. I had a student that came in the morning and presented in front of her friend and me. That was a huge step for her. We want to build an environment where all students feel comfortable speaking and sharing, but some just need a little more time to get there. It is important to remember that accommodating those students is better for them in the long run.

Those are four major areas of any ELA classroom, and 20 Time touches on them in different ways throughout the project. Nobody can suggest that 20 Time does not fit in with state or federal standards or whatever standards your district or school have adopted. Without a doubt, 20 Time helped improve the reading, writing, and speaking skills of my students, and anyone that saw their talks at the end of the year would know it as well.

How do you get administrators on board with a project of this scale?

This is always a tricky question to answer because every school and district have their own set of administrators and parents, and the teacher making a choice to implement 20 Time into their classroom needs to decide the best way to engage parents and administrators. I have found that there are three ways to engage administrators on 20 Time that may work for you and your situation.

1. Ask permission - This is the most straight forward approach to implementing 20 Time in your classroom, but it could also lead to the biggest issue. If you ask permission, the administrator might think there is something troublesome with the project

that requires administrator approval. Depending on the administrator, they might say no or put this on hold until a more in-depth meeting can be held. Sometimes, administrators can suck the passion out of a project. You have to have a good read on your administrator if you are going to ask permission.

2. Pilot it - One way to go about asking your administrator with a little less fear about saying no is to ask to run it as a pilot in your class. Show him this book and other 20 Time resources and say you want to try this in your class. Running pilots in districts and/or buildings is a pretty common practice, and 20 Time is the perfect type of program to run as a pilot. The nice thing about a pilot is that you need to run it for two to three years to get all of the data to make a decision on how 20 Time has impacted the learning of the students in class.

3. Just do it - I view 20 Time as just another assignment that happens to take a longer time to complete than others. I do not ask my administrator to allow me to do any other assigned work in my class. Why should I ask for permission? This is the approach I took for implementing 20 Time in my classroom. I just planned everything, rolled it out, and then I let the administrators know in passing they should come to my class and check out the work the students are doing. I believe my casual approach to introducing the idea to the administrators allowed them to go in with an open mind to learn what was going on in class. Seeing

engaged students is something that administrators are always looking to find in a classroom, and 20 Time provides that easily.

Every teacher needs to have a good understanding of what their administrator would and would not support. If you are new to a building and really want to try this, connect with your mentor and see if they can give you a read on the administrators in your building. They can help guide you through the process and offer the support you will need. Who knows, maybe you can get them to run 20 Time in their classes as well.

Does 20 Time work with students with special needs?

One of the best things about 20 Time is the flexibility it has built into the system. Since students are choosing the projects, they can choose whatever they want that matches their skillset. The fact that most of 20 Time is ungraded really empowers students with special needs because they can truly focus on the skills and not the grade. This is really true of any project that allows for student choice. The special education department loved having students in my class because the student choice aspect made it possible to differentiate for their students and ensure that their measurement of success was tailored to them.

The one part of 20 Time that might be difficult for students with special needs would be the unstructured nature of the 20 Time days. That independent work time might not be best for them. Students who struggle with that type of unstructured time were allowed to go to the resource room and get support for their project from the aides. It was nice to see them stay and engage with other students, but it was important that they went down and received the support they needed when it felt a bit overwhelming to them. 20 Time is about letting all students explore new ideas. It is one of the most inclusive types of projects you can have in the classroom.

What if a student doesn't do 20 Time?

There is always the fear that a student is not going to do the assignment. What's nice about 20 Time is that there is plenty of time for the teacher to touch base with students and support them if they are struggling to complete their work. Is it possible that some students can just fake their way through the entire project and not really learn anything from it? Yes. How is that different from any other assignment a teacher might give? Those students are few and far between, but they do happen. I have a great example of a student who did not take the project seriously but might have learned the most out of anyone in the class.

20 Time Missed Opportunity

A student in one of my American literature classes flew under the radar throughout 20 Time. He was active in class during 20 Time days and was a good student for the rest of the curriculum, but he was phoning in the project. As a teacher, it is easy to go back and be critical of some missed signs of his coasting, but also, I have 140 students, and these types of things can happen. However, it wasn't the fact that he did not take the project seriously that stands out. It was his talk at the end of the year that resonated with me.

He signed up for his speech to be near the end of the days available, and when he went up there, he was very honest. He said he did not take this seriously, that he hardly put any effort into the project, and this was a huge blow-off for them. Students were shocked at his honesty and were looking to me for a reaction. I was waiting for him to finish before passing judgment. I was glad I waited because there was a huge plot twist.

He said he was ready to completely blow off this presentation but changed his mind after seeing everyone talk so highly of their projects, and the different things they learned along the way. He said he realized that he just wasted one of the best opportunities he ever had to learn. He spent so much time not wanting to do school stuff, he missed his one chance to determine what school would look like for him. He said he learned to not waste your chances because you are stubborn or hardheaded. He basically said he learned so much from not doing anything.

This is an interesting take on not committing fully to 20 Time, but it showed the power of 20 Time in general by surrounding students with others that were working on their projects. I think there is one thing to keep in mind when it comes to this and any project—there is no such thing as the perfect project that will engage 100% of the students 100% of the time. There are going to be students that choose not to engage in the project, and it is the teacher's job to try and provide the best opportunity for students to learn and engage. We can't force the kids to do it, but we can create that environment where they can if they want. Don't beat yourself up if a student chooses not to embrace 20 Time. Talk with them, find out why they were resistant, and try to address any issues for similar students the next time around.

What if more than one teacher wants to do 20 Time?

This is one of those good problems to have. If you are doing 20 Time in your ELA class and a teacher in social studies also wants to do it, how does that work? If students are the same in both of those classes, are they working on the same project or different ones? This is a tough situation to have because you want more students to experience 20 Time, but multiple teachers doing it can create a logistical nightmare. If you have multiple teachers looking at using 20 Time as part of their class, then it might be time to have conversations about making 20 Time a class that all students take at some point during their time in school. As students get older, this can get progressively more difficult because schedules are much more complex. If you are in the middle or high school world, there might be a solution to this conundrum in the next chapter.

Final Thoughts on 20 Time and Genius Hour

Running 20 Time in my class is one of the best things I have ever done as an educator. I saw so many amazing students do so many amazing things. It is something I will always remember and something that students have thanked me for years later. Students experienced some of the most amazing things because I got out of their way and asked them what they wanted to explore. Empowering students to fully explore their passions and interests leads to amazing things. As a final part of this long chapter, I want to share one more story that came from a 20 Time project that is a great bit of advice for all of us.

What's Your Mountain?

Kitty came to me at the start of the 20 Time process and told me that her goal was to climb a mountain—well, not just any mountain, Mt. Kilimanjaro. In Africa. I smiled and thought that this was a great example of aiming high but being ok with not getting the goal. It's about the journey, not the destination. Kitty got to work doing tons of research and found a missionary group that did work at the base of the mountain and was able to get a final cost to make this happen. She was determined to raise all of the funds she could to make this dream happen. She made cookies and sold them at school. She made t-shirts and hosted her own day at school! She declared one day of the school year, "Climb Your Mountain Day" and encouraged everyone to find their proverbial mountain and climb it. She designed and screen printed all of the shirts herself. It was inspirational.

Fast forward to the end of the school year, and we are scheduling the times for the students to give their talks, and Kitty had to go first because she was scheduled for a flight to Florida to take her to Africa. She did it. She made this happen. She did missionary work at the base of Mt. Kilimanjaro and was able to climb it. When the next school year started, I had lunch with Kitty and told her I never thought she was going to pull it off. Her response sticks with me to this day: "I know. Nobody did. That's why I did it."

Teacher Reflection

How scared are you to hand over this much control to students? Explore the reasons you are scared below.

CHAPTER

8

ACTION RESEARCH PROGRAM

I am so lucky to be at a school that fully embraces the idea of PBL. They have embraced it so much, it has become a cornerstone of an amazing program that takes place in high school. The action research program (ARP) is dedicated to helping high school students understand how to do proper research, explore design thinking as a means to problem-solving, create artifacts to demonstrate understanding, and explore areas of learning that interest them. Think of it as a four-year process dedicated to preparing students for the best 20 Time project of all time! The ARP system has evolved over the years, and that is a good thing. Like PBL, ARP is flexible to the evolving needs of the students and staff. ARP is ingrained in grades 9–12 and looks like this.

Grade 9 ARP

This is a year-long, two-semester class that starts with the basics of research and design thinking. Students spend the year understanding what good sources are and how to find the best information available on a variety of subjects. They also explore design thinking as part of a process to improve their problem solving and critical-thinking skills. As part of the design thinking unit, students come down to the makerspace and are given a design challenge to accomplish. It is a fun way to engage the students in the process while allowing them to explore what the process means to them.

Another great aspect of this class is the focus on asking the right questions. I think many of us take for granted the ability to ask pointed questions to help get to the meat of an issue. Sometimes students stop digging after the first Google results page. Teaching students to explore using the right questions is a fundamental skill, and I love that our high school takes the time to include that in the ARP curriculum.

> *"Teaching students to explore using the right questions is a fundamental skill."*

ARP 9 also works with other content areas and connects curriculum. One of the connections includes ARP 9 and freshman English class. They work together to create a project that demonstrates the multidimensionality of characters from *The Merchant of Venice*. I was able to work with students and their projects for this unit, and the students created some amazing artifacts using the 3D printer and the laser cutter. This curriculum crossover takes place in the latter part of the second semester, so it is nice to see the students demonstrate their learning from the previous lessons of ARP and English to complete a great project for class.

Students	Teachers
Focus on asking the right questions.	Show students how to conduct in-depth research.
Learn to check the validity of sources.	Share the design thinking process.
Connect design thinking to other aspects of learning.	Support students as they explore PBL.

Grade 10 ARP

In grade 10, aspects of ARP are connected to the U.S. history course. The U.S. history course looks at important events in America through a local lens. The goal is to connect the history with who we are today in the community. This approach makes the history more relevant to the students and creates a greater sense of connecting to their pasts. Traditionally, history is played out in textbooks, film strips, and lectures. The local connections encourage our students to connect to the history of their parents and grandparents in a way that other history classes never did.

Another benchmark for the grade 10 ARP program is that the U.S. history class focuses on experiential learning. Students are up and moving and going on field trips whenever possible. As part of the unit on the Civil War and slavery, students visit the Second Baptist Church in downtown Detroit because it was a last stop on the Underground Railroad before many fugitive slaves made the crossing over the Detroit River to Canada and their freedom. Hearing stories and being in the same place as runaway slaves is a very impactful moment for these students. As schools moved more into the direction of testing, field trips fell out of favor because they were viewed as unnecessary expenditures. With the rise of Google Cardboard, AR, and VR, some think that the field trip is dead. Well, not in ARP 10. Students are up and out experiencing history in a wonderful hands-on fashion.

Students	Teachers
Immerse in experiences to have a better understanding of history. Explore how world events impacted the local community. Research and create artifacts that demonstrate an understanding of world and local events.	Create experiential learning opportunities for students. Connect a larger view of the world to a local view. Support students as they investigate world and local histories.

Grade 11 ARP

The grade 11 ARP program is a semester-long class that starts in the second semester of the school year. The focus for ARP 11 is to start to explore the different topics they might choose to focus on during their senior year. They also spend time learning how to narrow down their topic to find something manageable for their senior year.

I like the setup of ARP 11 because it is a good use of time to allow students to think about their senior-year project without spending too much time during senior year doing this. If I could have had students choose their 20 Time projects over the summer, that would have allowed more time to devote to the project itself. Using ARP to prime the pump for senior year is a wonderful way to get students thinking about this important project and allows them to further think about it over the summer. That time supports students who want to explore their ideas more deeply and possibly tweak them before school starts. Again, the emphasis on student ownership is key here because this is their topic, and they are responsible for choosing the topic and investing the time over the summer, gearing up for the work they will need to do.

Students	Teachers
Think about big-idea topics. Work with the teacher to narrow down a topic to fit the scope of ARP. Outline research needs for the project. Identify the types of artifacts that might be needed for the project.	Guide students as they explore possible topics. Help students narrow down their topics. Direct students to resources to support research on their topic. Connect students with experts in their field of study.

Grade 12 ARP

The grade 12 ARP class is a full-year class that is dedicated to the research of their topic and the creation of their artifact and presentation for the Celebration of Research event that happens at the end of the year.

Seniors work with their ARP mentor teachers on creating their projects and collaborate with other students or teachers as needed to support their work. They spend time in class bouncing ideas off one another and exploring options for their artifact creation. The new makerspace at our school that has 3D printers, laser cutters, VR equipment, and more has really opened the door to the types of artifacts that students can create for the Celebration of Research event. Here are just some of the student topics as I write this:

- Exploring near-death experiences
- Room design and Feng Shui
- Exploring Virtual Reality in medicine
- Designing facial prosthetics for special effects in movies
- Exploring the decline of woodworking classes in schools
- Facial reconstruction and 3D design

These are 17- and 18-year-old students that chose complex but interesting projects to explore, and they are all so excited to share their work when people ask about it. That type of engagement is something all teachers hope for when students choose projects.

Students	Teachers
Confirm the topic for their project.	Guide students to a single topic.
Connect with experts in the field of their topic.	Help students find the correct question to ask.
Pose a question.	Connect students to experts related to their topic.
Research possible answers/solutions to the question.	Help students organize their research and board.

	Rehearse presentations with students.
Create a board to showcase an understanding of the topic.	
Create an artifact to demonstrate an understanding of their topic.	

The Celebration of Research

The ARP ends with a Celebration of Research. At the end of the school year, students prepare for a multi-night event where the school doors are open, and the community can come and see all of the work students have been doing during their senior year. It is an awesome thing to see students lining the hallways of the entire school, showcasing their hard work. This formal event allows people from the community to ask questions and learn about the types of things students have been spending four years building. Each student has a professional board made up to showcase different aspects of their research, and they may also have additional artifacts they display. Think of this like a science fair, except this covers an area that the students were interested in exploring.

What is nice about the Celebration of Research is that students from all of the grades get to see what the seniors have been doing as well. Freshmen, sophomores, and juniors get a chance to see what it is they are building toward while in their different ARP classes. The middle school students also get a chance to tour the different projects in the school and see what high school will look like for them.

When the Celebration of Research is done, the research boards hang in the main lobby and hallways until the next year. I love coming into school and seeing all of these great examples of learning lining the hallways. It is a wonderful way to validate the work the students are doing by giving them a prominent display throughout the school.

Final Thoughts on the Action Research Program

The action research program is a fully embedded approach to PBL. This type of program is designed for high school, but I could easily see how it could be tweaked to make it work in middle school if a year-long, embedded program was desired at that level. ARP takes all of the amazing things of 20 Time and dedicates time over four years for students to not only just explore areas of learning that interests them but prepare them on how to research and ask the right questions. ARP takes the natural inquisitive nature of people and makes it part of the DNA of the school.

By embedding ARP into the school, the school is validating the idea that student interests are important and should be given time to be explored. Every school should not be designed to fill students with information to be spat back out on a state test but to nurture the curiosity that is inherent in all children. That nurturing will help create life-long learners who will be better prepared to tackle the big problems that life will throw at them in the future. For more information on ARP, check out http://bit.ly/ULiggettARP.

Teacher Reflection

What would you have explored in high school if given the time during the school year? What would be the first step at implementing something like ARP in your school?

CHAPTER

9

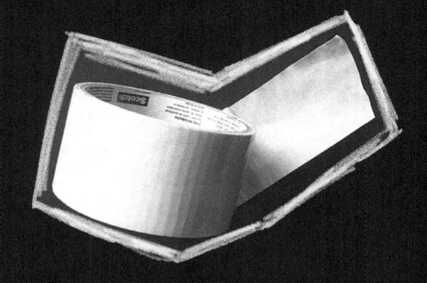

SUPPORTING
PROJECT- BASED
LEARNING

It is one thing to say that you believe in PBL, and it is another to support it through changes to the school and classroom environments. Active steps need to be taken so students have the right spaces and tools to work on their projects and feel supported in what they are trying to learn. Every school and district is different, so you might not need all of these options. You actually might have some of these resources but haven't thought about using them to support PBL.

Media Specialists

Librarians/media specialist are some of the most important people in any school or district. Sadly, they are some of the first people cut when schools are looking to trim the budget. This is a huge mistake. Media specialists are highly trained professionals that are the exact staff you need in schools today. As the Internet allows for more people to access more information, it is important to have someone who can help guide students and teachers through the murky waters of fact and fiction.

Media specialists are wonderful resources for students to use when they begin the research portion of any project. Librarians know where to find the best information on practically any topic. If they don't have the answer, they know where to look for it or whom to ask. It is critical that any teacher embracing PBL at its highest levels forms a strong partnership with the media specialist in their building. This partnership will allow you to work side by side to support students as they explore topics that interest them. With the extra help from a media specialist, every student can be supported as they work to demonstrate an understanding of the material covered in class.

Makerspace

Makerspaces hold a special place for me because building my first space really opened my eyes to what PBL could truly be. Part of PBL is using a variety of tools to demonstrate an understanding of the class material. Some students have access to a wide variety of tools at home and can create amazingly ornate projects to share with the class. Other students do not have that type of access. A makerspace helps bring some equality to the classroom when it comes to PBL.

As an ELA teacher, I am looked at strangely and asked by some people why I am interested in building a makerspace. "Those are for science and math teachers," they would tell me as I worked on writing grants and organizing information. PBL is something that has been in the sciences for a very long time. Labs are just projects that allow students the opportunity to demonstrate that they understand what was covered in class. There is no reason that other content areas, ELA, social studies, phys ed, etc., shouldn't be allowed to engage in PBL as well. A makerspace is just a space with different tools for anyone to create something in. If the students want to use the space to create an artifact to demonstrate an understanding of a concept covered in their U.S. history class, that is awesome. If they want to sit and knit a scarf for their *Doctor Who* cosplay outfit, that is fine too. We just need to give the students the space to create, and they will do amazing things with it.

Makerspace Tools

One of the things I often hear from people is a question about the types of tools that should go into a makerspace.

My standard response is to ask the students. They will tell you what they need, and those are the tools that should be in your makerspace. Having said that, here is a list of a variety of tools that can be found in makerspaces and are great tools for PBL.

littleBits

I love littleBits. Each bit is part of a circuit that you can build to accomplish something. Some can activate a fan, and others can provide a temperature. The bits snap together with magnets and do not require any soldering or coding. I gave a set to my son, and he was able to create a push-button flashlight. He put three bits together, and he was all set. He turned to me and said he could now find all of the things he lost under the couch. It's a simple and fun way to get started with making.

littleBits In Action

I have been a fan of littleBits for a while now, and it is because it is such a simple tool that allows students to explore how circuits connect. I like to have littleBits out in the open most of the time because it inspires students to just sit and tinker with them. They can learn and explore in the makerspace and not worry about being graded. Watching my young son use littleBits is what really inspired me to bring them to the school makerspace.

I opened up the box of littleBits at home and was checking them out to see what types of projects students could create with them in their science class. My son, six years old at the time, started to grab the bits and snap them together. He quickly snapped the battery, button, and LED bits together to create his own flashlight. He didn't follow any directions or set plan, he just snapped things together and made what he wanted.

He did the same with a temperature sensor, number bit, and fan. He snapped them all together with the battery and was able to read the temperature and have the fan kick on. He said he could use this at night when it got too hot. He planned to hold it over his face while he slept. Not the best plan for his invention, but his creation was amazing. He basically created a simplistic version of an air conditioning unit. If he connected it to the code bit and coded the fan to kick on only at a certain temperatures, he would be able to take that project to the next level.

Makey Makey

Have you ever wanted to play digital bongos with a banana? Of course, you have, and Makey Makey now lets you do that. With some jumper wires and one board, you can connect a directional pad and buttons to other objects and interact with your computer. I've seen students use Play-Doh, oranges, raspberries, pennies, and anything that is conductive to create gamepads. While these might not be practical uses of the wires, they teach the concepts of how wires can be used and how input and output work. Watching kids of all ages play with this is so much fun.

Makey Makey In Action

In sixth grade math, students were learning about the X and Y coordinates on a plane. Instead of spending a week staring at graphing paper, our math teacher had students create a game on Scratch that required them to move characters along the XY plane. As the students worked on their games, some were ready to take the next step and design their own controller. Using Makey Makey, students were able to create their own specialized game controller. This took the XY coordinate lesson to the next level for those students. By the end of the unit, students were able to demonstrate their understanding of the XY coordinate plane by having their teacher play the game they created on Scratch.

Raspberry Pi

Raspberry Pi is a $35 computer! Yes, you read that correctly. This computer is the size of a credit card that runs a full operating system. You connect to an HDMI monitor, add a keyboard and mouse, and you are ready to go. I became a Raspberry Pi Certified Educator, and I keep learning all of the cool things that can be done with Pi. You can run Scratch, you can play Minecraft, and you can program the Pi to do just about anything! Check out RaspberryPi.org for tons of resources on using Pi in the classroom.

Raspberry Pi In Action

As part of a design class, students were pushed to solve problems they identified in the local community. That local community could be defined as the school, town, or even state. One group of students thought they had the solution to the attendance issues at our school and were going to use the Raspberry Pi to solve it.

The students thought it might be easier for students and the teacher if they scanned their school IDs in and out of class instead of having the teacher takes attendance or give hall passes. It was an interesting take on a problem the school was having. The students dove in and started to write code and purchase a scanner to read the student IDs.

After a few months, they had a working prototype and presented it to the school superintendent. He was blown away at the idea and encouraged the students to refine the process and even gave the students school funds to continue the work!

While it would be later determined that the student project worked well, it was not financially feasible to roll out to every classroom between two high schools. The students were bummed, but they learned so much about coding and electronics through the process and were invested in it because it was their idea that they wanted to see all the way through. That is the beauty of PBL.

3D Printers

You might want to have students use 3D printers in your makerspace because you have seen them before and think they are very cool. Let me set the record straight—3D printers are really freaking cool. They are simply magic. I'm sure there is a bunch of science-y things and engineering things going on, but it is pure magic to watch a piece of jewelry printed right in front of your eyes. It is like watching something appear on the Holodeck or replicator on *Star Trek: The Next Generation*. I never thought it would be something I would see as commonplace, but they are, and your school can have one. However, there is much more to a 3D printer than printing random things.

The real power of 3D printing is not the printer, it is the design process. If you painted an awesome portrait and then placed it on a copy machine to make a copy, you did not learn anything from the copy. You learned while creating the original product. The same is true for 3D design and printing. The hours of hard work that can go into an original design can teach a user so much about geometry and physics. Learning to create something from scratch that adheres to basic design principles they discover on their own is a great learning tool for students. I've watched students struggle with creating the correct size and shape of objects so they would not topple over on the print bed. I've seen students struggle with their print job because they were designing in millimeters instead of inches. Students achieved a great understanding of these items through the design process not the printing process. That is the true power of 3D printers. It gives students another tool to learn new and valuable skills.

3D Printers In Action

This example of how the 3D printer has been used with PBL is one of my favorites. As part of a high school forensic science class, students were studying how facial reconstructions are completed. To give the students a chance to fully explore what this was like, we printed a dozen skulls for the students to practice their own reconstructions in class. Each skull took about 36 hours to print, but the students were given a chance to actually reconstruct what a person would have looked like based on the 3D printed skull. This is the type of project that students would not have been able to do in the past. A student in twelfth grade loved this so much, she chose facial reconstruction to be the basis for her ARP project. Since she has access to all of the tools at the school, she can focus on the research and create an amazing project at the end of the year. I can't wait to see her final work during the Celebration of Research.

Laser Cutter

I never thought I would see the day that would allow for laser cutters to be desktop sized, but here we are. Laser cutters, dedicated to fabrication, are advanced tools for a makerspace. This is not the type of purchase one usually makes at the beginning stages of building a makerspace, but it is a purchase to consider as your space grows and students start to consider more complex types of projects.

Laser cutters are perfect for a variety of projects and have been used in grades K-12. Depending on the model that you purchase (our space has a Full Spectrum Muse and a Dremel LC40), you can connect it to a window to vent directly outside, or you might have a filter that allows you to take the laser cutter wherever you want. Finding the right laser for your school environment should take time. This is not the type of purchase you want to rush.

Laser Cutter In Action

As part of an elementary project where students were learning about using money, the students were going to open their own lemonade stand in the school to practice making change. As part of this project, the teacher thought it would be nice for the students to have clearly marked coins as they worked on making change. The teacher worked to design special school-marked coins that the laser cutter would cut out for the students to use. It was awesome to see a teacher so invested in making something for their students and using the makerspace to make it happen. The students loved the coins, and the project was wonderful.

Craft Supplies

You need to stock the space with as much arts and crafts material you can get your hands on for the makerspace. No matter the age, students love to get crafty when it comes to projects. There are so many different uses for string, yarn, popsicle sticks, hot glue, construction paper, Play-Doh, duct tape, and so much more. Students are constantly in the space using a wide variety of these tools for miscellaneous projects. These tools can be found just about anywhere, and having them in a makerspace makes it easier for all students to access some of the tools many of us take for granted.

Power Tools

This one truly depends on the school. Some schools still have woodshop class, and a makerspace doesn't need to have these types of tools. My school does not have a woodshop class, and some of the work students wanted to do required the cutting and sanding of wood. So, I went out and bought a whole bunch of power tools for the makerspace. Circular saws, miter saws, table saws, saw saws, power drills, etc., were placed in one part of the makerspace designed for fabrication. I wasn't sure how the space would be used by students, but it did not take long for students and teachers to come up with some amazing projects that required the use of these tools.

It is important to note that the space with all of the tools is an adult supervision–required space. Students in middle school and high school know they are not allowed in that space without an adult present. Safety is always key for any space, and the makerspace is no different. On the flip side,

I have had the chance to help students learn to use tools for the very first time. It might sound crazy, but there are seniors in high school that have never used a power drill or any type of saw.

Power Tools In Action

At the high school I work at, we have a great engineering class that allows students to build something at the end of the semester. One year, the students were tasked with interviewing the robotics team and design and build items based on their wants and needs. This was a wonderful example of how a makerspace can be used to support students in their quest to demonstrate an understanding through the creation of an artifact. One group of students needed to create a battery cart to move their large batteries around from tournament to tournament. The students came in with their design and bought the wood but were not sure where to start. With a little guidance, students were off building their project. Students learned to use the nail gun, the miter saw, the level, and the power drill to build a top-notch cart for the robotics team. These students might not need to use any of these tools, but if they do, they will remember how because the teacher utilized PBL for the end of the year assessment.

CNC Machine

CNC machines are drills that are moved by a computer to carve our items from wood, plastic, metal, and other materials. These heavy-duty tools tend to be found in serious fabrication shops, but they are now more accessible to schools and hobbyists at home. The CNC machine uses designs created to carve shapes or engrave materials. It is a very loud tool, and they can take up lots of space. Our CNC machines (we have the desktop Carvey and the full-size X-Carve from Instructables) are kept in the fabrication space with the laser cutter because the room can be closed off to keep the sound down. Students in high school have found the CNC machine to be wonderful to use for small signage projects, but there has been increased use thanks to the engineering class, and usage will shoot up even more once the middle school design class starts.

CNC Machine In Action

For Chinese language class, students were tasked with designing their own stamps using Chinese characters. They chose their name and had to translate that into the Chinese characters and then arrange them so they could be read. From there, we entered the names into the CNC software, inverted them, and carved them on linoleum blocks to create stamps of their Chinese names. This is a perfect project for the beginning Chinese students as they learn the characters in the Chinese alphabet. Students were excited to see the X-Carve slowly trace out their characters and then carve them out of the blocks of wood for them to use. It led to lots of different ideas on how they might use CNC machines for future projects.

Minecraft Education Edition

Minecraft is popular in elementary and middle schools but still has a nice following in high school. The Minecraft Education Edition is the full Minecraft kids know and love plus special education features. Teachers can adjust the world settings and give students different materials to build with in their world. There is also a full chemistry set that allows characters to mix chemicals and see the mix's consequences. It is much safer to blow yourself up in Minecraft than it is in school. The education edition also allows users to code the world around them using text- or block-based code. Minecraft Education Edition is still growing and updating all of the time. It is a wonderful addition to any classroom, and that is why we have decided to roll it out in our K-12 school. We can't wait to see what the students will craft next.

Minecraft In Action

There are so many different examples that would fit here, but I think I am going to share the one that we will be doing next. The students will be exploring the Greek myths, and one of them will be about the Minotaur. Students will be tasked with creating their own labyrinth for other students and teachers to try and escape. This will be a fun way for students to work on their building skills and their research skills as they look to create a complex system of passageways and rooms to trick and confuse anyone daring enough to attempt to escape. With the coding features in Minecraft Education Edition, the creator of the world can teleport the player back to start as needed if they get too lost. This is the type of awesome tool-specific project that supports student learning to use a tool as well as other content-specific skills.

These are not all of the tools that make a makerspace a makerspace. You do not need all of these or even any of these. Your space needs to be tailored to the students in your school. Take it slow, and only get the items that students are requesting or that teachers already have plans to use in their classroom. The exciting thing about a makerspace is that it is designed to grow and evolve. Since our lessons should do the same, makerspaces and PBL are a match made in nerdom.

Teacher Reflection

What type of tools do you think students would use in your school if they had access? How might a makerspace help students who do not have access to a variety of tools? How might you utilize a makerspace with your students during a project-based lesson?

CHAPTER
10

FINAL THOUGHTS

You have made it all the way to chapter 10! Great job! PBL can be a scary endeavor. I want to give everyone some tips on how to get started implementing PBL into their classroom. You might not need all of these, but I think some of these are perfect for any teacher, no matter where they are in their educational journey.

TAKE A BREATH

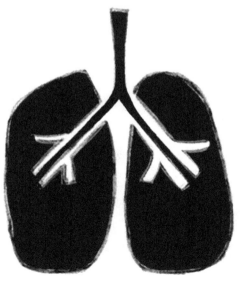

This is very important because you just finished a book and you are now filled with all of these crazy ideas of what you want to do next. I love it when teachers are excited and want to change the world one lesson at a time, but it needs to be tempered. Taking a moment to breathe and assess where you are at and where you want to go. That moment or two of calm can help set the stage for an amazing evolution of your classroom.

PICK A STARTING POINT

Pick a starting point - The last thing you want to do is approach project based learning from the standpoint of a complete and utter overhaul of your entire curriculum right away. That is nonsense. Any teacher who took that approach would rightfully be overwhelmed. **Choose one aspect of your curriculum** that you think would be perfect for project based lesson. Make that your starting point and see where it takes you.

REFLECT ON CHANGE

Reflect on change - As you start to make changes to your curriculum and embed project based learning more fully into your lessons, take the time to **reflect on what is working and what is not working.** These reflections are key because you are going to make mistakes and you do not want to make the same ones over and over again, so reflect often.

INCLUDE STUDENTS

Include students in the process - One of the scariest things any teacher can do is **ask for student feedback on projects or assignments.** We all fear the negative thoughts from our students and that is why we tend to ignore those type of evaluations. However, if you want to embrace project based learning, you need to know what is working and not working for them. Some of the best changes to different projects I've done in class came from student feedback.

TAKE A LEAP OF FAITH

Take a leap of faith - Sometimes, you just need to **go for it.** It can be scary and you can fail, but you have to trust the fact that you are an amazing educator dedicated to trying to find the best thing for your students. Let the students know you are trying something different and jump in. The worst that can happen is that the lesson is a bomb, but that is not the first time that has ever happened to any teacher, so do not let it stress you out. **Pick yourself up, dust yourself off, and try again.**

CELEBRATE

Celebrate your wins - When things go the way they are supposed to, celebrate! You have earned it. Most importantly, **celebrate so other teachers can see you.** Talk about the awesome work students are doing, invite administrators to see the projects students have created, take images and share them with parents on social media. **Spread the good word** because the more that people share the power behind project based learning, the more students around the world will get a chance to experience it as well.

My take on PBL is different than the average person's, but that is what I love about education and projects. We can take what we see, tweak them to make them work for ourselves and our students, and then share it to others so they can repeat the cycle. We are all in this together, so I hope you will take a leap of faith and see how PBL can change the way your students view learning.

Bibliography

"Gold Standard PBL: Essential Project Design Elements."
PBLWorks, Buck Institute for Education, 2019,
www.pblworks.org/what-is-pbl/gold-standard-pro-
ject-design.

CPSIA information can be obtained
at www.ICGtesting.com
Printed in the USA
BVHW070200281221
625039BV00005B/335